FOUR
VIEWS
ON

GOD AND CANAANITE GENOCIDE
SHOW THEM NO MERCY

Books in the Counterpoints Series

Church Life

Exploring Theology

FOUR
VIEWS
ON

GOD AND CANAANITE GENOCIDE
SHOW THEM NO MERCY

The Case for Radical Discontinuity: C.S. Cowles

The Case for Moderate Discontinuity: Eugene H. Merrill

The Case for Eschatological Continuity: Daniel L. Gard

The Case for Spiritual Continuity: Tremper Longman III

Stanley N. Gundry, series editor

COUNTERPOINTS
► CHURCH LIFE ◄

ZONDERVAN®

ZONDERVAN

Show Them No Mercy
Copyright © 2003 by C. S. Cowles, Eugene Merrill, Daniel Gard,
and Tremper Longman III

Requests for information should be addressed to:
Zondervan, *Grand Rapids, Michigan* 49530

Library of Congress Cataloging-in-Publication Data

Show them no mercy : four views on God and Canaanite genocide /
    C. S. Cowles . . . [et al.].
        p. cm. — (Counterpoints)
        Includes bibliographical references and indexes.
        ISBN 978-0-310-24568-1
        1. War — Biblical teaching. 2. Genocide — Biblical teaching. 3. Canaanites —
Biblical teaching. I. Cowles, C. S. II. Counterpoints (Grand Rapids, Mich.)
BS680.W2 S48 2003
230'.0411 — dc21   2002151808

Printed in the United States of America

HB 02.15.2024

CONTENTS

INTRODUCTION

Anyone who reads the Old Testament from cover to cover will encounter roadblocks to understanding its abiding message. All too often, for example, readers get bogged down in the latter half of Exodus and especially in Leviticus, asking themselves what relevance the "rule upon rule, precept upon precept" has for the Christian, especially since "it is for freedom that Christ has set us free [from the law]" (Gal. 5:1). If we were to excise these parts from our Bible, would we really miss anything?

An equally potential pitfall arises when readers encounter God's revealed law on war against the Canaanite nations (e.g., Deut. 20) and then how these rules were played out in, for example, Jericho (see Josh. 6:17–21). How could the God of the Bible command such an indiscriminate slaughter of an entire people, especially since in the New Testament Jesus commands us to love and to pray for our enemies? Our tendency is often to push this question into the backs of our minds and allow it to sit there, unresolved.

The authors of the various essays in this book seek to assist us in bringing this second issue to a resolution in our minds. As with many controversial matters in biblical interpretation, of course, they do not see eye to eye on how best to resolve the issue. All four of them, however, start from the basis of acknowledging the authority and inspiration of the Scriptures. On that theological foundation there is no disagreement.

The particular problem of biblical interpretation discussed in *Show Them No Mercy* has come to the forefront in recent years as many of us have learned a new word: *jihad*. Indeed, there is some correspondence in theme between the Muslim term *jihad* and the biblical expression *holy war* (or, perhaps better, *Yahweh war*). Not coincidentally, all four of the contributors make a passing reference to the events of September 11, 2001, when Muslim radicals, in the name of their religion and inspired by Osama bin Laden, destroyed thousands of innocent civilians. All civilized people abhor what happened on September 11; are we equally to abhor what happened in Jericho more than three millennia ago?

Moreover, in such places as Rwanda, Bosnia, and Kosovo, we have seen the indiscriminate slaughter of thousands of innocent civilians of a single ethnic group. We are now familiar with the terms *genocide* and *ethnic cleansing*—words that were not a part of our vocabulary a couple decades ago. The images we have seen on our television screens pull at our heartstrings and make us ask: What difference, if any, is there between modern ethnic cleansing and the Canaanite genocide sanctioned in the Old Testament text? If it is wrong in the twentieth and twenty-first centuries A.D., was it also wrong in the fifteenth or thirteenth centuries B.C. (depending on when one dates the conquest of Canaan)?

We hope that in some way the various essays provided in this book will help you bring about a resolution in your mind to this troublesome issue. Through it all, may God and his Word be glorified.

STAN GUNDRY, SERIES EDITOR

ABBREVIATIONS

ANET	*Ancient Near Eastern Texts*
BEATAJ	Beiträge zur Erforschung des Alten Testaments und des antiken Judentum
BETL	Bibliotheca ephemeridum theologicarum lovaniensium
Bib	*Biblica*
BibSac	*Bibliotheca sacra*
BJS	Brown Judaic Studies
BR	*Biblical Research*
BWANT	Beiträge zur Wissenschaft vom Alten und Neuen Testament
BZAW	Beihefte zur Zeitschrift für die alttestamentliche Wissenschaft
EvQ	*Evangelical Quarterly*
FOTL	Forms of the Old Testament Literature
FThS	Freiburger Theologische Studien
HAT	Handbuch zum Alten Testament
HBT	*Horizons in Biblical Theology*
HSM	Harvard Semitic Monographs
Int	*Interpretation*
JBL	*Journal of Biblical Literature*
JETS	*Journal of the Evangelical Theological Society*
JPSTC	The Jewish Publication Society Torah Commentary
JRE	*Journal of Religious Ethics*
JSOTSup	Journal for the Study of the Old Testament Supplement Series
KAT	Kommentar zum Alten Testament
NAC	New American Commentary
NCBC	New Century Bible Commentary
NICOT	New International Commentary on the Old Testament

NIDOTTE	*New International Dictionary of Old Testament Theology and Exegesis*
NIV	New International Version
NIVAC	NIV Application Commentary
OTL	Old Testament Library
PEQ	*Palestine Exploration Quarterly*
RB	*Revue biblique*
RevExp	*Review and Expositor*
SJT	*Scottish Journal of Theology*
SWJT	*Southwestern Journal of Theology*
TDOT	*Theological Dictionary of the Old Testament*
TOTC	Tyndale Old Testament Commentaries
TynBul	*Tyndale Bulletin*
VT	*Vetus Testamentum*
WBC	Word Biblical Commentary
WMANT	Wissenschaftliche Monographien zum Alten und Neuen Testament
WTJ	*Westminster Theological Journal*
ZAW	*Zeitschrift für die alttestamentliche Wissenschaft*

Chapter One

THE CASE FOR
RADICAL DISCONTINUITY

C. S. Cowles

THE CASE FOR RADICAL DISCONTINUITY

C. S. Cowles

Should any believe it his duty to reply hereto, I have only one request to make—Let whatsoever you do, be done inherently, in love, and in the spirit of meekness. Let your very disputing show that you have "put on, as the elect of God, bowels of mercies, gentleness, longsuffering," that even according to this time it may be said, "See how these Christians love one another!"

John Wesley, Preface, Sermon on "Free Grace"

When the LORD your God brings you into the land you are entering to possess and drives out before you many nations . . . then you must destroy them totally . . . and show them no mercy.

Do not leave alive anything that breathes. Completely destroy them . . . as the LORD your God has commanded you.

(Deut. 7:1–2; 20:16–17; see Deut. 7:3–5; 20:16–18; 32:39; Josh. 6:21; 8:24–26; 10:28, 40; 11:11, 14, 20–21)

You have heard that it was said, "Love your neighbor and hate your enemy." But I tell you: Love your enemies and pray for those who persecute you, that you may be sons of your Father in heaven.

(Matt. 5:43–44; see Matt. 5:45–48; Luke 6:27–36; 9:51–56)

Amid the hopes, dreams, and lives shattered when the twin spires of America's cathedral of capitalism crashed to the ground on September 11, 2001, was evangelicalism's easy accommodation with Old Testament genocidal "texts of terror."[1] This was played out on full camera when Jerry Falwell, making an appearance on *The 700 Club*, reflexively attributed the deadliest terrorist attack on Americans in history to God's judgment. He blamed "pagans and abortionists and the feminists and the gays and the lesbians . . . the ACLU, People for the American Way, all . . . who have tried to secularize America."[2]

In the wake of the media furor that followed, including a White House official who made it clear that "the president does not share those views,"[3] Falwell issued an apology in which he totally reversed himself. "Neither I, nor anyone else, has any reason to believe that the terrorist-inflicted atrocities of September 11 have anything to do with the judgment of God," he averred, "and I should not have stated otherwise. Our Lord is a God of love. He proved it ultimately and forever when He sent His Son, Jesus Christ, to die on the cross for all sinners, including me."[4] Robertson's Christian Broadcasting Network released its own statement, calling Falwell's on-air remarks "severe and harsh in tone" and explaining that the show's host, Pat Robertson, who had initially agreed with Falwell, had not "fully understood" what Falwell had said.[5]

Falwell and Robertson unwittingly found themselves impaled on the horns of a dilemma that has vexed biblical interpreters since the formation of the canon of Christian Scripture: How do we harmonize the warrior God of Israel with the God of love incarnate in Jesus? How can we reconcile God's instructions to "utterly destroy" the Canaanites in the Old Testament with Jesus' command to "love your enemies" in the New Testament? The short answer is: with great difficulty.

---

[1]Cf. Phyllis Trible, *Texts of Terror* (Philadelphia: Fortress, 1984).

[2]*Newsweek* (Sept. 24, 2001), 7; *USA Today* (Sept. 18, 2001), 13A.

[3]*Washington Post* (Sept. 14, 2001), C03.

[4]*USA Today* (Sept. 21, 2001), 23A.

[5]*USA Today* (Sept. 18, 2001), 13A.

TENSION BETWEEN TEXTS

Commitment to the inerrancy and infallibility of *all* Scripture[6] leaves evangelical biblical scholars and theologians little choice but to maintain the "tension between the texts" cited above, by asserting that both statements are to be regarded as equally true. They argue that the indiscriminate annihilation of the Canaanites was indeed willed by God even though, as John Bright points out, "it tells a bloody tale of battle, violence, and wholesale slaughter, a slaughter in which God assists with his mighty acts; the smoke of burning towns and the stench of rotting flesh hangs over its pages." He adds, "It is a story of fanaticism, of holy war and wholesale sacrificial destruction (the *ḥerem*)."[7] To attribute such atrocities to the actual intention and will of God, however, poses insuperable difficulties for Christian theology, ethics, and praxis.

That the issue of divinely initiated and sanctioned violence is no mere academic matter was tragically demonstrated in the self-destructive insanity that decimated Rwanda, the most Christianized nation in Africa, when the dominant Hutus set out to exterminate the minority Tutsis. In one hundred days, Hutus brutally slaughtered nearly 800,000 Tutsis and Tutsi sympathizers. Peter Gourevitch recounts the horrific scene that unfolded at the Seventh-day Adventist Mission Hospital complex in Mungonero, where two thousand beleaguered Tutsis took refuge in the early days of the massacres.[8]

Dr. Gerard, a United States–trained physician and the hospital administrator, welcomed them and then sealed the perimeter. On April 15, 1994, he announced: "Saturday, the sixteenth,

---

[6]The doctrine of scriptural infallibility and inerrancy was spelled out by three hundred fundamentalist and conservative evangelical biblical scholars, theologians, and pastors in *The Chicago Statement* of 1978. It affirmed, in summary, that "God, who is Himself Truth and speaks truth only, has inspired Holy Scripture," that "being God's own Word ... [it] is of infallible divine authority in all matters upon which it touches," that "being wholly and verbally God-given, [it] is without error or fault in all its teaching," and that "the authority of Scripture is inescapably impaired if this total divine inerrancy is in any way limited or disregarded, or made relative to a view of truth contrary to the Bible's own."

[7]John Bright, *The Authority of the Old Testament* (Grand Rapids: Baker, 1978), 243.

[8]Philip Gourevitch, *We Wish to Inform You That Tomorrow We Will Be Killed with Our Families: Stories from Rwanda* (New York: Farrar Straus & Giroux, 1998), 26.

at exactly nine o'clock in the morning, you will be attacked."
Scarcely able to believe their ears, seven Tutsi Seventh-day
Adventist pastors wrote a hasty letter to their district president,
Pastor Elizaphan Ntakirutimana, who happened to be Dr. Ger-
ard's father. They pleaded for him to intervene "the same way
as the Jews were saved by Esther." He sent back a curt reply:
"You must be eliminated. God no longer wants you."[9]

At 9:00 A.M. on Saturday, Dr. Gerard drove up to the hospital complex with a carload of armed Hutu militia. Nearby Hutu
villagers brought their machetes and joined in the attack. They
slowly and methodically killed all those who had crowded into
the chapel, then the school, and finally the hospital. The seven
Tutsi pastors prayed with their people until they too were cut
down. Early the next morning, Dr. Gerard led the militia to the
nearby village of Murambi, where other Tutsi survivors had
taken refuge in the Seventh-day Adventist church. They killed
them all.

The mind reels. The stomach retches. How can any human
being, much less those who declare their allegiance to the Prince
of Peace, engage in such atrocities? Yet the sad fact is that the
history of the church is as blighted by such bloodshed as that of
Israel and Islam. Christians took up the sword against Muslims,
Jews, and other "infidels" during the Crusades. Protestants and
Catholics slaughtered each other in the "holy wars" that tore
Europe apart following the Reformation. The Roman Catholic
Church tortured, burned, drowned, and flayed hundreds of
thousands of supposed heretics and witches across more than
five centuries of the Inquisition. Christian Europeans not only
forcibly seized aboriginal lands but destroyed 80 percent of
North and South America's native populations by genocide, disease, and drunkenness during the bloody era of colonial aggression and aggrandizement. And it was ostensibly the most
Christianized nation in Europe that systematically shot, gassed,
and burned six million Jews in the Nazi Holocaust.

We hang our heads to admit it, but *jihad* ("holy war") is not
a Muslim invention. Its origins and justification are to be found
in the Hebrew Scriptures. Moses was the first in known history
to spell out an ideology of "holy war" that dictated—unlike
Muhammad's reformulation—the genocidal destruction of ene-

---

[9]Ibid., 28, 42.

mies. Moses and Joshua were the first to engage in campaigns of "ethnic cleansing" as *ḥerem* ("acts of religious devotion"). It is to these texts that Christians have appealed, from St. Augustine in the fourth century to Orthodox Serbs in the twentieth, in justifying the mass destruction of human beings. Paul knew from his own pre-Christian experience how easily the Word of God can be perverted to justify unspeakably violent acts when he wrote, "The letter kills" (2 Cor. 3:6).

Even that pales, however, next to the spiritual and emotional damage caused by grotesquely distorted concepts of God engendered by genocidal passages. Most evangelical commentators, following Moses, justify the "ethnic cleansing" of the Canaanites "on account of the wickedness of these nations" (Deut. 9:4). Such "radical surgery" was necessary in order to purify the land of "all the detestable things they do in worshiping their gods" (Deut. 20:18).[10] In his commentary on Joshua, John Calvin states that God "was pleased to purge the land of Canaan of the foul and loathsome defilements by which it had long been polluted."[11] He admits that the

> indiscriminate and promiscuous slaughter [of the Canaanites], making no distinction of age or sex, but including alike women and children, the aged and decrepit, might seem an inhuman massacre, had it not been executed by the command of God. But as he, in whose hands are life and death, had *justly doomed* those nations to destruction, this puts an end to all discussion. [emphasis added][12]

Justly doomed? What could possibly be "just" about the wanton and indiscriminate slaughter of "women and children, the aged and decrepit"? Insofar as Calvin's theological presuppositions would allow no other conclusion but that God had willed it from before the foundation of the world, he caught

---

[10]"A surgeon does not hesitate to remove an arm or a leg, or even a vital organ, when life is at stake. The very existence of Israel—and ultimately the salvation of the world—depended upon [it]" (William Sanford LaSor, David Allan Hubbard, and Frederic William Bush, *Old Testament Survey*, 2d ed. [Grand Rapids: Eerdmans, 1996], 147–48).

[11]John Calvin, *Commentaries on the Book of Joshua*, trans. Henry Beveridge (Edinburgh: Calvin Translation Society, 1855), 97.

[12]Ibid.

himself and acknowledged that "*the decree is dreadful indeed*, I confess" (emphasis added).[13]

"Dreadful" is a gross understatement. John Wesley declared that to attribute such atrocities to God is an outrage against his character and makes him "more false, more cruel, and more unjust than the devil.... God hath taken [Satan's] work out of [his] hands.... God is the destroyer of souls."[14] Theologian Walter Wink protests, "Against such an image of God the revolt of atheism is an act of pure religion."[15]

Regarding people such as Wesley and Wink, who contend that Moses' genocidal commands make a mockery of God's justice, not to mention his holiness and love, Peter Craigie responds in *The Problem of War in the Old Testament*: "The participation of God in human history and through human lives does not primarily afford us a glimpse of his moral *being*; it demonstrates rather his will and *activity*."[16] To which one might ask: How else is God's "moral *being*" demonstrated apart from "his will and *activity*"? Is not the one who steals a thief? The one who commits adultery an adulterer? The one who kills a killer? To attribute genocidal violence to God poisons the well of all his other attributes. Wesley points out that "it directly tends to destroy that holiness which is the end of all the ordinances of God. It overturns ... his justice, mercy, and truth."[17]

Given the way distorted concepts of God are being acted out in the religiously incited violence of our time, brought shockingly home on Black Tuesday, September 11, 2001, evangelicals no longer have the luxury of defending genocidal "texts of terror" as reflective of either God's "moral being" or his "will and activity." Nor is there any need to do so. John Bright reminds us that the Old Testament "is a document of the faith of old Israel, and only secondarily a document of the church. Its message is not of and by itself a Christian message."[18] Walter Brueggemann

---

[13]John Calvin, *Institutes of the Christian Religion*, ed. John T. McNeill, trans. Ford Lewis Battles (Philadelphia: Westminster, 1960), 3.23.7 (pp. 955–56).

[14]John Wesley, "Free Grace," in *The Works of John Wesley* (London: Wesleyan Conference Office, 1872; repr. Kansas City: Nazarene Publishing House, n.d.), 7:373–86.

[15]Walter Wink, *Engaging the Powers* (Minneapolis: Fortress, 1992), 149.

[16]Peter C. Craigie, *The Problem of War in the Old Testament* (Grand Rapids: Eerdmans, 1978), 42.

[17]Wesley, "Free Grace," 7:376, 382

[18]Bright, *The Authority of the Old Testament*, 183.

cautions that "Old Testament theological articulation does not conform to established church faith.... There is much that is wild and untamed about the theological witness of the Old Testament that church theology does not face."[19]

There is a better way of dealing with the conflicting divine commands regarding the treatment of enemies. It is to acknowledge what is everywhere assumed in the New Testament, namely, that while there are vast and vitally important areas of continuity between Israel's faith and that of the church, there are significant instances of radical discontinuity as well, none more so than in reference to divinely initiated and sanctioned violence. There were good reasons why the church fathers, in settling upon the canon of sacred Scripture, separated the Hebrew Scriptures from the Christian and gave to the former the designation "old" and the latter "new."

In so doing, they were following the precedent set within the New Testament itself. Paul drew a sharp distinction between the "old covenant" embodied in the Torah and the "new covenant" personified in Christ. The former "was fading away," while the latter is endowed with "ever-increasing glory" (2 Cor. 3:7–18). The author of Hebrews goes even further in his assertion that "by calling this covenant 'new,' [God] has made the first one obsolete; and what is obsolete and aging will soon disappear" (Heb. 8:13).

Over against the testimony of many Old Testament texts that reflect what Martin Luther called "the dark side of God" is the clear and unambiguous testimony of John, who exults, "God is light; in him there is no darkness at all" (1 John 1:5). He goes even further to state categorically that "God is love [*agapē*]" (4:8). James's exuberant witness is that God is "the Father of the heavenly lights, who does not change like shifting shadows" (James 1:17). Paul exults that we no longer see "a poor reflection [of God] as in a mirror" (1 Cor. 13:12), but "with unveiled faces" we behold the full "glory of God in the face of Christ" (2 Cor. 3:18; 4:6).

NEW WINE, OLD WINESKINS

The equilibrium of the physical world is periodically interrupted by what physicist James Clerk Maxwell called "singular

---

[19]Walter Brueggemann, *Theology of the Old Testament* (Minneapolis: Fortress, 1997), 107.

points." A tiny seed-crystal dropped into a saturate solution will turn the whole mass into a similar crystalline form. A drop in temperature of one degree can cause the waters of a mighty ocean to freeze over. Splitting one atom may precipitate an explosive chain reaction of unimaginable force. Likewise, says Maxwell, in human affairs "there are unpredictable moments when a small force may produce, not a commensurate small result, but one of far greater magnitude, the little spark which kindles the great forest, the little word which sets the whole world a-fighting."[20]

Human history moves along lines of relative continuities until a singular point emerges, after which a sea change in thinking and behavior occurs. It may be triggered by an event as seemingly insignificant as taming fire, fashioning a wheel, or reducing language to writing. It may be focused in a person such as Abraham, Plato, or Copernicus. When that event occurs or person emerges, no matter how unremarkable at the time, everything changes. Nothing will ever again be the same.

The birth of Jesus is more than just one more singular point among many. It is so uniquely singular that it has become the axial point of human history. It signals that moment when divinity intersected humanity in a way analogous to what physicists describe as the point of absolute singularity from which the universe emerged. This is the truth that the evangelist John proclaims when he begins his Gospel by linking these two points of singularity: "In the beginning was the Word, and the Word was with God, and the Word was God. He was with God in the beginning. Through him all things were made" (John 1:1–3). He who was present and active at the event-moment of the so-called "Big Bang" and who directed all subsequent stages of creation is incarnate in Jesus of Nazareth (John 1:14–18). This is the astonishing faith claim that lies at the heart of Christianity.

Jesus was not one prophet of Israel among many. He was not just another voice crying in the wilderness. In his person, message, and mission, Jesus embodied and proclaimed an exhilarating and yet disturbing new revelation. Claims were made by him and of him that radically set him apart from all who

---

[20]As quoted in Lewis Mumford, *The Conduct of Life* (New York: Harcourt, Brace & World, 1951), 227.

came before. After acknowledging that "in the past God spoke to our forefathers through the prophets at many times and in various ways" (Heb. 1:1), the author of Hebrews goes on to say that "in these last days he has spoken to us by his Son, whom he appointed heir of all things, and through whom he made the universe. The Son is the radiance of God's glory and the exact representation of his being" (1:2–3). Never before had any "forefather" or "prophet" been called "the Son" of God. Never before had it been claimed that a human being exhibited "the radiance of God's glory," much less that he embodied an "exact representation of [God's] being." Clearly, Jesus represents a whole new order of divine disclosure. Between him and all who came before, there is an infinite qualitative difference.

In his Pentecost sermon, Peter drew a sharp contrast between "the patriarch David [who] died and was buried" and Jesus, whom "God . . . raised" (Acts 2:29, 32). The resurrection decisively set Jesus apart from all who came before. It was God's definitive "Yes," reaffirming his word spoken to Jesus at his baptism, "You are my Son, whom I love; with you I am well pleased" (Mark 1:11). Though there was no one of antiquity venerated more highly by the Jews than Moses, the author of Hebrews asserts that "Jesus has been found worthy of greater honor than Moses. . . . Moses was faithful as a servant in all God's house. . . . But Christ is faithful as a son over God's house" (Heb. 3:3–6).

No word of Scripture ever claimed that Moses or Joshua was "taken . . . into heaven" or "exalted to the right hand of God" (Acts 1:11; 2:33). Jesus outranks Moses, Aaron, Joshua, and even the angels: "So he became as much *superior* to the angels as the name he has inherited is *superior* to theirs" (Heb. 1:4, emphasis added; see 1:5–14; 3:1; 4:8–10; 5:4–6). John likewise attests to the radical discontinuity between the old and the new covenants: "For the law was given through Moses; grace and truth came through Jesus Christ" (John 1:17).

The uniqueness of Jesus as the divine Son of God is dramatically portrayed in the Transfiguration account. Appearing with him were the two greatest figures in Israel's religious history: Moses, the primal mediator of God's law, and Elijah, the prototypical prophetic spokesman for God. Yet only Jesus was transfigured. It was not to these two seminal figures of the old covenant that the heavenly voice was directed but to Jesus: "This is my Son, whom I love. Listen to him!" After that, the three disciples whom Jesus had taken along with him "looked around [and], they no longer saw anyone with them except Jesus" (Mark 9:2–8). This is one of the clearest texts showing that the revelation of God in and through Christ at once fulfilled and superseded "the Law and the Prophets" (Matt. 7:12).

Paul made the distinction between the old and the new covenants even more pronounced. "Now if the ministry that brought death ... came with glory, so that the Israelites could not look steadily at the face of Moses because of its glory, fading though it was, will not the ministry of the Spirit be even more glorious?" There is a pronounced difference between "the letter [that] kills," "engraved in letters on stone," and "the Spirit [that] gives life," a "glory of that which lasts." The "veil" that had for so long shrouded the old covenant, obscuring the radiant beauty of God's glory, "in Christ is ... taken away." The happy result is that "we, who with unveiled faces all reflect the Lord's glory, are being transformed into his likeness with ever-increasing glory" (2 Cor. 3:6–18). And what is that glory? "The glory of *Christ, who is the image of God*," "the glory of *God in the face of Christ*" (2 Cor. 4:4, 6, emphasis added). All that the "fathers" and the "prophets" under the old covenant had seen dimly and understood partially is now fully and finally disclosed without distortion in Jesus.

Jesus presents us with an accurate "image [reflection, refraction] of the invisible God," because in him "all the fullness of the Deity lives in bodily form" (Col. 1:15; 2:9). When Philip asked Jesus to "show us the Father," Jesus responded, "Don't you know me, Philip, even after I have been among you such a long time? Anyone who has seen me has seen the Father" (John 14:8–9). In the New Testament, Jesus is not defined by God; rather, God is defined by Jesus. Jesus is the lens through whom a full, balanced, and undistorted view of God's loving heart and gracious purposes may be seen. What is *new* about the new covenant is that *God is like Christ*. "To see what God is like," says Philip Yancey, "simply look at Jesus."[21]

---

[21]Philip Yancey, *Reaching for the Invisible God* (Grand Rapids: Zondervan, 2000), 125.

In his life, death, and resurrection, Jesus literally and figuratively ripped the temple's great veil in two, "destroyed the barrier, the dividing wall of hostility" (Eph. 2:14). He let us see with astonishing clarity that the essential attribute of God's heart, the fundamental character trait from which all divine activity proceeds, is what John Wesley called "holy love."[22] No longer should Christians define God as the "God of Abraham, the God of Isaac and the God of Jacob" (Ex. 3:6), as important as they were in salvation history, but as the "Father of our Lord Jesus Christ, the Father of compassion and the God of all comfort" (2 Cor. 1:3). Hans Küng speaks of God as having a "human face," the face of the human being, Jesus of Nazareth. He goes on to say that the God of Jesus is "unequivocally good and not evil.... God is not indifferent, but friendly to man. Jesus calls him good, alone good, merciful."[23]

Wesleyan theologian Thomas A. Noble rightly suggests that the starting point in forming a truly Christian theology is not what the Bible teaches about God in general but what Jesus reveals about God in particular.

> Theology is ... only truly *theocentric* if it is *Christocentric*. It is not, as Donald Baillie reminded us, theism with Christology tacked on. There is no knowledge of God except "through the light of the gospel of the glory of Christ, who is the Image of God," no knowledge of the Father except through the Son, so that our theology then must be *Christonormative*.[24]

If this is the case, then God is not like the first Joshua, a warrior, but like the second, the Prince of Peace.[25] As the anonymous Christian writing to Diognetus put it, "violence is no attribute of God."[26]

---

[22]Mildred Bangs Wynkoop, *A Theology of Love: The Dynamic of Wesleyanism* (Kansas City: Beacon Hill, 1972), 24.

[23]Hans Küng, *On Being a Christian*, trans. Edward Quinn (Garden City, N.Y.: Doubleday, 1976), 300, 304.

[24]Thomas A. Noble, "The Knowledge of the Glory of God," in *The Tower*, ed. Harold E. Raser (Kansas City: Nazarene Theological Seminary, 1997), 1:19.

[25]Joshua and Jesus share the same Hebrew name, *Yeshua*.

[26]*The Epistle to Diognetus* 7.4, in *The Apostolic Fathers*, ed. Kirsopp Lake (Cambridge, Mass.: Harvard Univ. Press, 1970), 374.

When someone preaches a sermon after which the listeners seek to kill him, one can safely assume that the preacher has touched a sensitive nerve. That is precisely what occurred when Jesus delivered his inaugural sermon at Nazareth (Luke 4:16–30). What was it about his reading of Isaiah's prophetic song that so infuriated the people? For openers, he stopped his reading before getting to the prophetic punch line, which represented the hopes and dreams of an aggrieved and oppressed people, namely, the long anticipated "day of vengeance of our God" (Luke 4:18–19; see Isa. 61:1–2).

The entire sweep of Jesus' life and death makes it abundantly clear that his editing of this Scripture passage was not accidental but intentional and that it represented an entirely new way of thinking about God. What Jesus was introducing was nothing short of an entirely new rewrite of Jewish theology. It would not be "off the wall" but drawn from the deep artesian springs of the Law and Prophets. It would constitute a sweeping recasting of God's gracious purposes, not only for Jews but for all humankind. It would be the fulfillment of the ancient covenant that in Abraham "all peoples on earth will be blessed" (Gen. 12:3). It would introduce the shocking, unprecedented, and utterly incomprehensible news that God is nonviolent and that he wills the well-being of all humans, beginning with the poor, the oppressed, and the disenfranchised.

To reinforce the fact that he intentionally amended the Isaianic text, Jesus focused attention on two obscure people mentioned almost in passing in the Hebrew Scriptures. Both were foreigners and idol worshipers (Luke 4:25–27). It did not sit well with Jesus' listeners to be reminded that it was a Baal-worshiping Sidonian widow, descended from Sidon, Canaan's eldest son—and thus under Noah's curse—who became a recipient of God's gracious miracle of continuing sustenance. Even less did they want to be reminded that, even though "there were many widows in Israel in Elijah's time" who had undoubtedly lost sons, it was not to these but rather to this despised foreign woman that God displayed his boundless compassion by raising her dead son to life in response to Elijah's earnest entreaty (1 Kings 17:22).

The God disclosed in Jesus and testified to in the Hebrew Scriptures is no respecter of gender, religion, or nationality. He is especially attentive to widows and children. Though the Sidonians were despised by the Israelites, who would have annihilated them if the tribe of Asher had carried out its assignment, they were precious in God's sight and worthy of his favor, and one of them received of his miracle-working power. Noah may have placed a curse upon the Sidonians through Canaan, but God did not.

This was too much for the solid citizens of Nazareth to accept. They were not ready to hear about a God who has no interest in balancing the scales of justice by an avalanche of destructive wrath, who bears no grudge toward their historic enemies. They could not comprehend a God whose love is boundless, whose care extends to a woman and her child living in an idolatrous culture and whose healing mercy embraces untouchables such as Naaman. Luke records that "all the people in the synagogue were furious when they heard this." Obviously, something had to be done about this rebel son, this blasphemer, this one who dared to take such interpretive liberties with their sacred Scriptures. "They got up, drove him out of the town, and took him to the brow of the hill on which the town was built, in order to throw him down the cliff" (Luke 4:28–29).

Something new was going on that would be dangerous to the old. From their ancient sacred texts Jesus mined truths about God that the Jews were unwilling to face. He drew out of the old scriptural wineskins a new kind of revelational wine. He lifted the veil that had blinded his generation from comprehending the magnanimous scope of God's love. He pulled aside the curtain that had hidden the *shalom*, the peace of God, that would embrace not only the Jews but all nations, until the whole earth would be filled with the glory of the Lord (cf. 2 Cor. 3:14–18).

The most incisive critique of God as destroyer occurs in the context of Jesus' final journey to Jerusalem (Luke 9:51–56). Jesus and his traveling party were not permitted to lodge in Samaritan territory because he was heading toward Jerusalem. The historic and bitter animosity between Jews and Samaritans cut both ways. James and John, to whom Jesus had previously given the name "Sons of Thunder" (Mark 3:17), responded typically by asking, "Lord, do you want us to call fire down from heaven to destroy them?"

Undoubtedly, they were thinking about Sodom and Gomorrah. They were ready to consign all of Samaria to destruction because of the inhospitality of a few. Apparently, it never crossed their minds that not only would the recalcitrant males perish but women, children, and the infirm, the very people whom Jesus had come to redeem. They would have thereby annihilated the woman at the well, who became the gospel's first evangelist, as well as the very people who would be the first beyond Judea to receive and welcome the good news of Christ's resurrection and the first to experience an outpouring of the Holy Spirit after Pentecost.

Jesus not only rebuked his disciples for entertaining such a thought but replied, "You do not know what kind of spirit you are of, for the Son of Man did not come to destroy men's lives, but to save them" (Luke 9:55[27]). Jesus made it crystal clear that the "kind of spirit" that would exterminate people was totally alien to his heavenly Father's character. The vengeful spirit that dehumanizes, depersonalizes, and demonizes a whole town or city or nation is not of God. The God revealed in Jesus never has been and never will be party to genocide of any sort, for "God is love" (1 John 4:8). "God did not send his Son into the world to condemn the world," John reminds us, "but to save the world through him" (John 3:17).

God does not have to judge sinners proactively because "whoever does not believe stands condemned already.... This is the verdict: Light has come into the world, but men loved darkness instead of light because their deeds were evil" (John 3:18–19). Those who do not believe in the Son are allowed to exercise their moral freedom and are left in their natural state of spiritual darkness and death (cf. 3:36).

This accords with Paul's analysis of how "the wrath of God is ... revealed from heaven against all the godlessness and wickedness of men who suppress the truth by their wickedness" (Rom. 1:18). The key phrase that appears three times in his exposition of humankind's downward spiral into depravity is "God gave them over" (1:24, 26, 28). God stepped back and allowed sin to run its self-destructive course. God's love was experienced as wrath when humans "exchanged the truth of God for a lie"

---

[27]See NIV text note. This part of verse 55 is not contained in all manuscripts, but it is contained in some of the older manuscripts.

(1:25; see v. 23) and thus bound themselves to that which God hates. Thus, they slipped ever deeper into the black hole of idolatry, sensuality, perversion, debauchery, and finally "death" (Rom. 6:23). Their fate was a self-chosen destiny.

The "destroyer" is not God but sin. Death came into the world through sin, which is inherently self-destructive (Gen. 2:16–17; Rom. 5:12–21). Aristotle offered a useful analogy. He pointed out that truth is linear; no matter how far you press it or when and where you touch it, it always remains consistent with itself. Falsehood, on the other hand, is circular; give it enough rope, and it will hang itself. If sin is "self-curved in upon itself," as Luther maintained, then sin contains within itself the seeds of its own destruction. God's wrath "is not retaliatory" nor "vindictive," according to Mennonite theologian C. Norman Kraus, but "points to the objective, intrinsic consequences of sin in the created order as God's judgment. The very concept of a rational creation implies an order of existence in which consequences are inherent in the actions themselves."[28]

God has committed final judgment into the hands of Jesus (John 5:22, 27; Acts 10:42; 17:30–31). Jesus is the one, as Michael Lodahl points out, who "has walked in our shoes and shared in our human lot.... Jesus, the divine Son who shares fully in our humanity, and who fully exemplifies what it is to be truly human, is thereby fully qualified to be the Standard or Judge by whom all people are measured."[29] God's attitude toward sinners is best seen in how Jesus treated Judas. Even though Jesus knew what was in his heart and what he was about to do, he loved him to the end. His love was expressed through gentle warnings, by making him the guest of honor at the Last Supper, in offering him first of all the cup of forgiveness, and by greeting him in the garden of betrayal as "friend" (Matt. 26:50). Judas died violently, not by God's hand, but by his own.

It is surely a fact of inexhaustible significance that Jesus never used his supernatural miracle-working power to hurt, maim, coerce, conquer, or destroy. He was the embodiment of God's servant, who "will not shout or cry out, or raise his voice in

---

[28]C. Norman Kraus, *God Our Savior: Theology in a Christological Mode* (Scottdale, Pa.: Herald, 1991), 210–11.

[29]Michael Lodahl, *The Story of God: Wesleyan Theology and Biblical Narrative* (Kansas City: Beacon Hill, 1994), 230.

the streets. A bruised reed he will not break, and a smoldering wick he will not snuff out" (Isa. 42:2–3). The God revealed in and through Jesus is not one who summons his "warriors to carry out [his] wrath" (13:3); much less does he will the indiscriminate genocidal annihilation of any peoples or nations. He is, rather, "the God of peace" (Rom. 15:33; Phil. 4:9; 1 Thess. 5:23; 2 Thess. 3:16; Heb. 13:20). It is not "holy warriors" who will be called "sons of God" but "peacemakers" (Matt. 5:9).

The God portrayed in the Old Testament was full of fury against sinners, but the God incarnate in Jesus is not. "For God so loved the [ungodly, wicked sinners]," exults John in the golden text of Christian devotion and theology, "that he gave his one and only Son, that whoever believes in him shall not perish but have eternal life" (John 3:16). God is "not wanting anyone to perish, but everyone to come to repentance" (2 Peter 3:9).

When Peter, in his abortive attempt to defend Jesus in the Garden of Gethsemane, cut off the ear of the high priest's slave, Jesus rebuked him: "No more of this!" (Luke 22:51). Then he restored the slave's severed ear in a gracious act of healing. Jesus directly countermanded Moses in forbidding the use of violence of any sort when he said, "Put your sword back into its place ... for all who draw the sword will die by the sword" (Matt. 26:52). Peter must have taken Jesus' rebuke to heart, for decades later he wrote, "Christ suffered for you, leaving you an example, that you should follow in his steps.... When they hurled their insults at him, he did not retaliate; when he suffered, he made no threats. Instead, he entrusted himself to him who judges justly" (1 Peter 2:21–23).

The earliest Christians were so sure of the nonviolent nature of God as revealed in Christ that they renounced all forms of violence, including military service, for the first three centuries of the church's existence. To be a disciple of Christ meant a commitment to "overcom[ing] evil with good" (Rom. 12:21). Tertullian held that love of enemies is the "principal precept" of Christianity and that "Christians would, like their Master, rather be killed than kill."[30] Their mission was not to conquer but to convert, not to destroy but to heal, not to recriminate but to reconcile—the polar opposite of Israel's Great Commission to anni-

---

[30]Roland Bainton, *Christian Attitudes Toward War and Peace: A Historical Survey and Critical Re-evaluation* (New York: Abingdon, 1960), 73, 76.

hilate all the peoples in the land of Canaan. For the sake of their convictions and because they would not fight back, uncounted multitudes of believers were led like lambs to the slaughter in wave after wave of persecution. Yet, armed with no rhetoric other than the gospel of peace and no weapons but love, these followers of the Prince of Peace eventually conquered Rome, their most vicious adversary, without drawing a sword.

When comparing the activities of the Israelites throughout their long history with that of early Christians, it is clear that theology matters and that people's concept of God makes a vast difference in terms of how they relate to one another and their world. It is the difference between ideologies of coercive and destructive violence embodied in the Islamic doctrine of *jihad* ("holy war") and the noncoercive, life-ennobling, self-giving love of God exhibited in Jesus on the cross.

Jesus not only renounced the use of violence but went to the unprecedented extreme of commanding love for enemies. Under the old covenant the rule and practice was, "Love your neighbor and hate your enemy" (Matt. 5:43). While "love your neighbor" is a scriptural command (Lev. 19:18), "hate your enemy" is not. Yet Israel's xenophobic and violent history bears sad witness to the fact that those beyond their religious and racial boundaries were regarded as other, as alien, as ungodly, as moral polluters, as the enemy, and thus as objects of boundless hate.

Over against a bloody history saturated with violence, believed to be divinely initiated and sanctioned, Jesus issued a new commandment that was as astonishing as it was radical: "But I tell you: Love your enemies and pray for those who persecute you" (Matt. 5:44). In this unprecedented pronouncement, Jesus said something that no prophet or priest ever uttered. His love ethic directly countermanded Moses' genocidal commands, predicated as they were on loathing the enemy.

On what basis did Jesus make such a nonscriptural, impractical, and impossible command? His startling answer was "that you may be sons of your Father in heaven. He causes his sun to rise on the evil and the good, and sends rain on the righteous and the unrighteous.... Be perfect [in love for enemies], therefore, as your heavenly Father is perfect [in love for enemies]" (Matt. 5:45–48). What Jesus introduced was an entirely new way of looking at God. God does not hate sinners or despise foreigners; much less does he desire their annihilation. He loves them with boundless and unconditional, self-giving love. He bestows his gracious "sun" of life and "rain" of favor on the just and the unjust, on those who love him and those who hate him. His love is "perfect": that is, it is all-encompassing, whole, complete, life-giving, life-sustaining, life-enhancing, and life-affirming for all humankind. Reflecting the creative and redemptive heart of God, Jesus said, "I have come that they may have life, and have it to the full" (John 10:10).

If ours is a Christlike God, then we can categorically affirm that God is not a destroyer. Death was not a part of God's original creation, neither will there be any more "death or mourning or crying or pain" in the new (Rev. 21:4). God does not engage in punitive, redemptive, or sacred violence. Violence and death are the intrinsic consequences of violating God's creative order; they are the work of Satan, for he was a "murderer from the beginning" (John 8:44). God does not proactively use death as an instrument of judgment in that death is an enemy, the "last enemy" to be destroyed by Christ (1 Cor. 15:20–28). And God does not deal with the enemy.

The sharpest point of discontinuity between the Old and New Testaments is evident in their starkly differing attitudes toward children. Moses made no exception for women and children in his command to "destroy [the Canaanites] totally" (Deut. 7:2; see v. 16). The narrator of the Conquest dispassionately reports that the Israelites "devoted [Jericho] to the LORD and destroyed with the sword every living thing in it—men and women, young and old" (Josh. 6:21). Typical of the subsequent accounts of Joshua's systematic extermination of the citizen populations of conquered cities is this summation: "He left no survivors. He totally destroyed all who breathed, just as the LORD, the God of Israel, had commanded" (10:40). Samuel's genocidal command to King Saul to "totally destroy" the Amalekites specifically spelled out "women, children and infants" (1 Sam. 15:3).

Not so Jesus! "Who is the greatest in the kingdom of heaven?" asked his disciples. Jesus answered that question by calling "a little child and had him stand among them." A child, for Jesus, is the epitome of the kind of person who will "enter the kingdom of heaven." How one treats children is how one treats Jesus, for "whoever welcomes a little child like this in my name welcomes me." Jesus directed his strongest invective against the one who would in any way harm a little child: "It would be better for him to have a large millstone hung around his neck and to be drowned in the depths of the sea" (Matt. 18:1–6). While Moses, Joshua, Samuel, and Herod the Great destroyed children, Jesus blessed them and said, "The kingdom of heaven belongs to such as these" (19:14).

Elie Wiesel, Nobel Prize–winning author and Holocaust survivor, gives us a haunting first-person account of what the genocidal destruction of Canaanite children may well have looked like. He describes his soul-searing experience of what he saw at sixteen years of age after being unloaded from a railway cattle car and marched into the camp at Auschwitz.

> Not far from us, flames were leaping up from a ditch, gigantic flames. They were burning something. A lorry drew up at the pit and delivered its load—little children. Babies! Yes, I saw it—saw it with my own eyes ... those children in the flames. (Is it surprising that I could not sleep after that? Sleep had fled from my eyes.)
>
> Never shall I forget that night, the first night in camp, which has turned my life into one long night, seven times cursed and seven times sealed. Never shall I forget that smoke. Never shall I forget the little faces of the children, whose bodies I saw turned into wreaths of smoke beneath a silent blue sky.[31]

Can we imagine Jesus at the wheel of that truck, backing it up and pulling the lever that dumps living children and babies into the flames? Can we image the God revealed fully and finally in Jesus ordering the killing of children and infants? At any time? In any place? For any reason?

BEYOND DISCONTINUITY

Few theologians have operated from the presupposition of the inerrancy of "all Scripture" as rigorously as Dutch Reformed theologian A. van de Beek. In Why? On Suffering, Guilt, and God, he takes the received text of both Old and New Testaments as representing the literal words of God. Thus, all distinctions

---

[31]Elie Wiesel, Night, trans. S. Rodway (Avon Books; New York: Hearst, 1960), 42–43.

between the Testaments are erased, and the differing historical locations, perspectives, and personalities of the human mediators of God's self-disclosure mean nothing. In that all parts of the Bible have equal weight of revelatory value, he must of necessity portray God as not only good and faithful but changeable, unpredictable, irrational, and even evil. "The way of God does not answer to our norms of good and evil.... God is a rough God, grim, and in our eyes even cruel.... God is not one you can figure out. Majestically he goes his own way.... Good and evil both come forth from his will."[32] One must learn to live with the fact, van de Beek argues, that "the more one wants to let all of Scripture speak for itself ... the more unclear the Bible becomes. The more we believe that the whole Word is revelation, the less we know who God is."[33]

If van de Beek's description of God is taken as normative—and it is faithful to a literal reading of the text—then how can we speak of Jesus as the embodiment of deity when he not only fails to incarnate Israel's image of a warrior God, from whom "good and evil both come forth," but discloses its exact opposite? In what sense can it still be claimed that the Father and the Son share the same essential nature? Does not such a view drive a wedge between God the Father and God the Son? Does it not undermine the deity of Jesus and shatter the historic doctrine of the Trinity? Sensing that the reader may well be frustrated by what appears to be a hermeneutic of "theological nihilism," van de Beek admits, "we could perhaps restrict revelation to certain events in the world. We could restrict it to certain texts in Scripture. But then what is the criterion for our selection?"[34]

John Wesley would answer in a flash: Jesus! As the full and final revelation of God, Jesus is "the criterion" for evaluating Scripture, the prism through which the Hebrew Scriptures must be read. Mildred Bangs Wynkoop succinctly capsules Wesley's Christological hermeneutic when she says: "Love *is* the gospel message. Christian love, *revealed by God in Christ* ... stands against any human ... theory of God's nature and His way with

---

[32]A. van de Beek, *Why? On Suffering, Guilt, and God,* trans. John Vriend (Grand Rapids: Eerdmans, 1990), 274–78.

[33]Ibid., 278.

[34]Ibid.

[35]Wynkoop, *A Theology of Love,* 18.

[36]Wesley, *Works,* 9:430.

man ... love as it is revealed in Christ" (emphasis added).[35] "It is well that you should be thoroughly sensible of this," said Wesley. "The heaven of heavens is love. There is nothing higher in religion: there is, in effect, nothing else."[36]

If we take love as it is revealed by God in Christ as our criterion for interpreting Scripture, then the "tension between texts" can be transcended. The "furious opposites," to use G. K. Chesterton's colorful phrase,[37] reflective in so many areas of discontinuity between the Testaments, find their resolution and unity in Jesus, the very one who seems to shatter them apart. This becomes clear in Jesus' own use of the Hebrew Scriptures, which he interpreted in light of his own self-understanding. He infuriated his Jewish opponents by declaring that the Scriptures existed primarily to bear witness to him. To the Pharisees he said, "You diligently study the Scriptures because you think that by them you possess eternal life. These are the Scriptures that testify about me.... If you believed Moses, you would believe me, for he wrote about me" (John 5:39, 46). When the risen Christ joined the two grieving disciples on the road to Emmaus, he asked, "'Did not the Christ have to suffer these things and then enter his glory?' And beginning with Moses and all the Prophets, he explained to them what was said in all the Scriptures concerning himself" (Luke 24:26–27).

While Jesus affirmed the Hebrew Scriptures as the authentic Word of God, he did not endorse every word in them as God's. He rejected some Torah texts as representing the original intention and will of God, such as Moses' divorce laws (Mark 10:4–9). He displaced Moses' laws governing vengeance with his new ethic of active nonviolent resistance, of "overcom[ing] evil with good" (Matt. 5:38–42; Rom. 12:21). His command to "love your enemies" (Matt. 5:44) represents a total repudiation of Moses' genocidal commands and stands in judgment on Joshua's campaign of ethnic cleansing. In his word of absolution to the woman taken in adultery, Jesus contravened the clear injunctions of the Torah calling for adulterers to be put to death (John 8:1–11; cf. Lev. 20:10; Deut. 22:22). It is clear that Jesus exercised an audacious prophetic authority over the Torah and on how it was to be interpreted.

[37]Cited by Philip Yancey in "Living with Furious Opposites," in *The Best Christian Writing, 2001*, ed. John Wilson (San Francisco: HarperCollins, 2001), 323.

Though Jesus did not "come to abolish the Law or the Prophets" (Matt. 5:17), it is apparent in the series of six antitheses that immediately follows—"You have heard it said.... But I tell you ..." (5:21, 27, 31, 33, 38, 43)—that his way of fulfilling them was to recast them according to the law of love (Matt. 22:34–40). The pronouncement "I tell you" appears thirty-two times in Matthew. It was, notes William Greathouse, "a unique aspect of Jesus' own authoritative speech, affirming but relativizing the Law."[38]

A sea change occurred, quite spontaneously and without any formal deliberation, in the earliest church's presuppositions regarding the grounds of divine revelation and scriptural authority. Although they continued to read, preach, and cite the Hebrew Scriptures as the Word of God, they did so primarily to prove that Jesus was indeed the long-anticipated Messiah of God. In that the Word had become flesh in Jesus, they now read and interpreted the Scriptures through the lens of Jesus illumined by the "Spirit of truth" (John 15:17). The bench mark of divine revelation in the era of the new covenant was no longer the Word of God mediated by Moses but by Jesus.

This hermeneutical change was so radical and offensive to unbelieving Jews that they hounded Jesus to the cross, stoned Stephen while accusing him of speaking "words of blasphemy against Moses and against God" (Acts 6:11), and harassed Paul to the end of his days. Ironically, the apostles never saw themselves as speaking "words of blasphemy against Moses." To the contrary, they grounded the good news of Jesus in "Moses and all the Prophets," even as the risen Christ had done when conversing with the two disciples on the Emmaus road (Luke 24:27). Yet the Jews could clearly see that by reading the Torah and Prophets through the prism of the person and work of Christ, they were changing the center of gravity of revelatory authority in fundamental ways.

First-century Jews, as well as orthodox Jews today, were triply insulted: Christians co-opted their sacred Scriptures in what has been called the biggest corporate takeover in history; then they labeled them as "old"; and finally they set aside major parts of it as no longer relevant for their faith and life. It was pre-

---

[38]William Greathouse, *Wholeness in Christ: Toward a Biblical Theology of Holiness* (Kansas City: Beacon Hill, 1998), 182.

cisely this shift that forced the Jews to expel the nascent Christian community from Judaism, a rupture that persists to this day.

The priority and finality of Jesus as the embodiment of God's love—and thus the one through whom the Scriptures are to be read—is evident in Wesley's exposition of the Sermon on the Mount:

> With what authority does he teach! *Not* as Moses, the servant of God; *not* as Abraham, his friend; *not* as any of the Prophets; nor as any of the sons of men. It is something more than human; more than can agree to any created being. It speaks the Creator of All! A God, a God appears! Yea, "I AM," the Being of beings, the self-existent, the Supreme, the God who is over all, blessed for ever![39]

Wesley's Christological hermeneutics come into sharp focus in his exposition of the proof text often cited to show that Jesus accepted the authority of every part of the Hebrew Scriptures: "Do not think that I have come to abolish the Law or the Prophets; I have not come to abolish them but to fulfill them" (Matt. 5:17). Wesley pointed out that when it came to "the ritual or ceremonial law . . . containing all the injunctions and ordinances which related to the old sacrifices and service of the Temple, our Lord indeed did *come to destroy, to dissolve, and utterly abolish*. To this bear all the Apostles witness" (emphasis added). He adds, however, that "the moral law, contained in the Ten Commandments, and enforced by the Prophets, he did not take away".[40]

That Jesus came "to destroy, to dissolve, and utterly abolish" large sections of the Torah is indeed a strong statement. Yet Wesley held that this was precisely what the New Testament witnesses believed Jesus had done. In his comment on the next verse, "not the smallest letter, not the least stroke of a pen, will by any means disappear from the Law until everything is accomplished" (Matt. 5:18), Wesley transposed the "letter of the law" into the word of Jesus: "His is a word of authority, expressing the sovereign will and power of Him that spake; of Him whose word is the law of heaven and earth, and stands fast for ever and ever."[41] Jesus' lordship extends over the entire cosmos

[39]Wesley, *Works*, 5:250–51.
[40]Ibid., 5:311.
[41]Ibid., 5:313.

from creation to consummation—and over the Hebrew Scriptures as well. As the preexistent Son of God and now resurrected and glorified living Word, Jesus is *the* Word for those who bind themselves to him.

Evangelicals of all theological persuasions acknowledge that in spite of the pervasiveness of divinely initiated and sanctioned violence in the Old Testament, there is no support in the New for imaging God as one who wills the indiscriminate slaughter of human beings, much less is he pleased when conquered peoples are offered up to him as *herem*, that is, as human sacrifices. In his discussion of "Holy War" in *Zondervan Handbook to the Bible*, Colin Chapman observes that "New Testament writers never think of military conquest as a way of furthering the cause of God. They think instead of the peaceful spread of the good news about Jesus Christ."[42] If we believe that Jesus is truly "the image of the invisible God" (Col. 1:15), then we must resist all efforts to defend Old Testament genocidal commands as reflective of the will and character of God. Since Jesus has come, we are under no obligation to justify that which cannot be justified, but can only be described as pre-Christ, sub-Christ, and anti-Christ.

Yet as offensive and as problematic as these texts are, they are part of the church's received canon of sacred Scripture and cannot simply be dismissed, although in practice that is precisely what the church has done. It has given genocidal texts a wide berth in liturgy, preaching, and Bible reading. Yet when such texts must be dealt with, many expositors from Origen in the third century to Duane L. Christensen today cut through the literal-historical outer husks of the narrative to uncover the hidden kernel of spiritual truth contained therein.

Origen, who was the first to produce a Christian commentary on the entire Hebrew Scriptures, was convinced, according to Joseph T. Lienhard, "that the whole Old Testament is a prophecy of Christ and of all that Christ signifies, and that Christ is the key to understanding the Old Testament. . . . Thanks to

---

[42]Colin Chapman, "Holy War," in *Zondervan Handbook to the Bible* (Grand Rapids: Zondervan, 1999), 230.

[43]Joseph T. Lienhard, "Origen and the Crisis of the Old Testament in the Early Church," in *The Best Christian Writing, 2001*, ed. John Wilson (San Francisco: HarperCollins, 2001), 182.

spiritual interpretation, the church freed itself from Judaism without having to reject the Old Testament."[43] By the use of allegory, analogy, and typology, Origen was able to find testimony to Christ—and thus spiritual edification—in virtually every chapter and verse of the Old Testament, even in texts that not only violate the teachings of Jesus but all human sensibilities, such as the genocidal commands.

Though such "spiritual interpretation" has often been widely criticized for its subjectivism and wild flights of fancy, exegetes still utilize it when trying to draw something of spiritual value out of patently non-Christian texts. In his exposition of Deuteronomy 7:1–2, for instance, Duane Christensen admits that "the concept of 'Holy War' is offensive to the modern reader because it suggests the barbarism of the Crusades of medieval times, or the *jihad* of Islamic fundamentalists." After categorically declaring war to be "inherently evil," he transitions immediately from Moses' clear-cut command to "destroy [the Canaanites] totally" to "the theological and psychological principles implied in this text."[44] He sees the battle scenes recounted in Joshua as a metaphor of spiritual warfare. "It is this spiritual battle to which this text speaks. To enter the promised land one must trust God to defeat the forces of evil. . . . As we engage the foe in spiritual battle, we must constantly be aware of the fact that it is God who fights in our behalf."[45]

Another way of dealing with the discontinuity between the Testaments is by utilizing the rubric of "progressive revelation" or "dispensationalism." We see this unfolding movement within the Hebrew Scriptures themselves in reference to sacrifices. While large sections of the Torah are devoted to divine commands regarding the detailed performance of sacrifices, Isaiah in speaking for God protests, "'The multitude of your sacrifices—what are they to me?' says the LORD. 'I have more than enough of burnt offerings, of rams and the fat of fattened animals; I have no pleasure in the blood of bulls and lambs and goats'" (Isa. 1:11).

---

[44]Duane L. Christensen, *Deuteronomy* (WBC; Dallas: Word, 1991), 32.
[45]Ibid.

This approach acknowledges that God accommodated his self-disclosure to the narrow limits of human understanding and historical context. Calvin asks:

> For who even of slight intelligence does not understand that, as nurses commonly do with infants, God is wont in a measure to lisp in speaking to us? Thus such forms of speaking do not so much express clearly what God is like as accommodate the knowledge of him to our slight capacity.[46]

"What we witness in the pages of the Bible," says Colin Chapman, "is the gradual process by which God works in the history of a particular people for whom war is an essential part of the religion and culture. By doing so he transforms these ideas to enable all humankind to understand more clearly the nature of the world we live in."[47]

It would be more accurate to describe this movement as the progressive *understanding* of God's self-disclosure. The problem of partial and even distorted concepts of God in the Old Testament has never been on God's side but on the side of the human mediators of that revelation. It was their "slight capacity," as Calvin pointed out, that limited their ability to comprehend the fullness of God's character and nature, which would come to light only in Jesus. As they received more light, their view of God correspondingly changed.

In 2 Samuel 24:1, for instance, we read that "the anger of the LORD burned against Israel, and he incited David against them, saying, 'Go and take a census of Israel and Judah.'" Curiously, when David obeyed the word of the Lord, he was "conscience-stricken ... and he said to the LORD, 'I have sinned greatly in what I have done'" (24:10). God's command becomes even more inexplicable when we read that "the LORD sent a plague on Israel," in which "seventy thousand of the people ... died" (24:15).

The postexilic Chronicler, however, resolved this glaring discrepancy by a small but significant emendation of the text: "*Satan* rose up against Israel and incited David to take a census

---

[46]Calvin, *Institutes of the Christian Religion*, 1.13.1, cited in Jack B. Rogers and Donald K. McKim, *The Authority and Interpretation of the Bible* (San Francisco: Harper & Row, 1979), 108.

[47]Chapman, "Holy War," 234.

of Israel" (1 Chron. 21:1, emphasis added). That a significant development in the understanding of God's role in the abortive census had occurred is obvious. The Jews had begun to project some of the darker attributes of Yahweh onto a contradivine being, Satan. We see this development most clearly in the book of Job. It was not God who caused the disasters that befell righteous Job, as both he and his comforters believed, but Satan.

In 1990, shortly after the Hubble Space telescope was launched, it was judged to be a five-billion-dollar boondoggle. Instead of sharp and clear pictures of the heavens, the images beamed back to earth were blurred, distorted, and virtually useless. The telescope simply would not focus properly. The problem was found to be in its principal light-gathering mirror. It had been ground with exquisite precision but in the wrong shape. A lengthy investigation traced the disaster to a simple, dumb mistake. A technician had assembled a device that guided the mirror-grinding process with one bolt put on backward. The resulting defect was so slight as to be calculated in thousandths of an inch. Yet it was sufficient to virtually ruin the telescope's revelational mission. It cost three critical years of viewing time and seven hundred million dollars for a complex array of corrective mirrors to be designed, manufactured, flown into orbit, and installed in the most complex space maneuvers by astronauts up to that time.[48]

There was nothing wrong with the revelatory light that has filled the heavens and the earth with the glory of God from the beginning, but there was something terribly wrong with fallen humankind's light-gathering capacity. Because of darkened minds and hardened hearts as a result of the curse of sin, the glory of God mediated under the old covenant had in some respects become so diminished as to be corrupted into what Paul calls "the ministry that condemns," even "the ministry that brought death" (2 Cor. 3:7–9).

Jesus came to pull back the curtain and let us see the beautiful face of God, "full of grace and truth" (John 1:14). Before he could reconcile us to God, he had to show us a loving heavenly Father to whom we would want to be reconciled: a God who is *for* us rather than *against* us, a God of love and grace who can be loved in return. Jesus came to remove the cataracts from our

---

[48]*Time Magazine* (Nov. 20, 1995), 90–99.

eyes because of sin, pierce the night of our dark distortions, and let us see "the glory of God in the face of Christ" (2 Cor. 4:6).

We must hasten to add that the mediators of God's self-disclosure under the old covenant were telling the truth as they understood it. That their understanding of the "truth" may have been flawed is evident in the way the genocidal command was limited and in how it kept changing. The divine order to "completely destroy" applied only to the peoples inhabiting the land of Canaan, not "cities that are at a distance" (Deut. 20:10–17). The criteria for annihilating the one and not the other had nothing to do with moral or religious issues but only that the former occupied the land the Israelites believed to be theirs.

The original command to "not leave alive anything that breathes" (Deut. 20:16), including animals, was scrupulously carried out in the sack of Jericho. Israel's subsequent rout before the Ai defenders and the severity with which they dealt with Achan's sin underscores how seriously they took that command. Yet from the conquest of Ai forward, only the conquered peoples were destroyed, not animals and personal effects: "Israel did carry off for themselves the livestock and plunder of this city, as the LORD had instructed Joshua" (Josh. 8:24–27). In that "livestock and plunder" were of value to them, the scope of God's annihilating command was conveniently moderated. Tragically, that shift revealed the inversion of moral values exhibited by the Israelites at that time: Animals were more highly valued than humans.

Even more curiously, in his rash treaty with the Gibeonites, Joshua was not reprimanded for having directly contravened God's clear command to "wipe out all [Canaanite] inhabitants" (Josh. 9:24), nor did Israel suffer battlefield defeats because of his disobedience. Achan perished for his sin and disobedience, but Joshua did not. It could be that God kept changing his mind about his genocidal will. More likely, Joshua's perception of what God was telling him to do kept changing according to the exigencies of the moment.

Attributing the command to annihilate Canaanites to God can be partly explained by the fact that the Israelites had no concept of Satan prior to the Babylonian exile. Thus all things—life and death, sickness and health, blessing and cursing—were seen as coming directly from the hand of the Sovereign Lord (see Deut. 28; 32:39–42; Ps. 44:1–19; Isa. 13:9–16). In addition, the Israelites believed the Canaanites to be under an ancient curse originating with Noah (see Gen. 9:24–27). Given the fact that the Canaanites were an idolatrous and morally degenerate people and were squatters on land long before promised to the patriarchs, it is understandable how the Israelites could have interpreted God's command to occupy the land in violent and even genocidal ways. Thus, in good faith they acted on what they believed to be God's will. The record clearly reports that God honored their obedience. What God required under the old covenant is the same that he requires today: not perfect understanding but a perfect heart of obedience.

That a radical shift in the understanding of God's character and the sanctity of all human life occurred between the days of the first Joshua and the second Joshua (i.e., Jesus) is beyond dispute. It was nothing less than moving from the assumption that God hates enemies and wills their annihilation to the conviction that God "so loved [enemies] that he gave his one and only Son" (John 3:16). As Wesleyan expositors Jack Ford and A. R. G. Deasley point out in their commentary on Deuteronomy 7:1–2:

> To apply these [genocidal] commands to warfare today would be a gross misapplication of scripture. There can be no doubt that, armed with the Christian gospel and endued with the Holy Spirit, Paul would have entered Canaan as he entered Corinth to show God's triumph over evil in transformed lives.[49]

This raises a critical question regarding the inspiration and authority of the Old Testament: If Moses and Joshua misunderstood the will and purposes of God in reference to the Conquest, then what parts of God's self-disclosure in the Old Testament can we trust? The question is moot if we ask the same of all who feel under no obligation to abide by Old Testament laws governing Sabbath worship, ritual circumcision, animal sacrifices, eating pork, charging interest, and capital punishment for adulterers and those who pick up sticks on the Sabbath. If Bible-believing Christians are asked how they can justify setting aside

---

[49]Jack Ford and A. R. G. Deasley, *Beacon Bible Commentary* (Kansas City: Beacon Hill, 1969), 539–40.

great blocks of divine commands in the Old Testament as "truth for today," even the most avowed scriptural literalists among them respond: because we are no longer living under the old covenant but the new. Exactly!

What we are suggesting is that we extend this functional Christological principle of biblical interpretation, employed by virtually all evangelicals, to cover texts of violence that are incompatible with the nature and character of God as disclosed in Jesus. What makes a Christian a Christian as opposed to a Jew, at least in part, is precisely this Christocentric orientation toward the Hebrew Scriptures. In opposition to Marcion, who sought to dispense with the Old Testament altogether, believers from apostolic times to the present take its testimony and counter-testimony with all seriousness, especially since "these are the Scriptures that testify about [Jesus]" (John 5:39). Yet at the same time, they affirm that the full and final self-disclosure of God's true nature and character is to be found "written not with ink but with the Spirit of the living God, not on tablets of stone but on tablets of human hearts" (2 Cor. 3:3). The central and ultimate purpose of "the holy Scriptures," claims Paul in another context, is "to make you wise for salvation through faith in Christ Jesus" (2 Tim. 3:15).

Our final authority, not only in matters of faith and salvation but in determining the true nature and character of God, is Jesus, to whom the Scriptures give faithful and true witness. Calvin taught: "It is Christ alone on whom ... faith ought to look. ... This ... is the proper look of faith, to be fixed on Christ."[50] John Stott reminds us that "our Christian conviction is that the Bible has both authority and relevance ... and that the secret of both is Jesus Christ."[51] Rather than sinners being exterminated, children being dashed to pieces, and wives being raped in the day of the Lord's "coming, cruel, with fury and burning anger," as envisioned by Isaiah (Isa. 13:9–16, NASB), God in Christ was violently seized, beaten, and crucified. Instead of destroying sinners, God allowed himself in his Son to be slain *by* sinners and *for* sinners on the cross. "God made him who had

---

[50]John Calvin, *Commentary on John 14:1* (Calvin Translation Society; *CO*, 47:64d.). As cited in Rogers and McKim, *The Authority and Interpretation of the Bible*, 107.

[51]"The Quotable Stott," *Christianity Today* (April 2, 2001), 64.

no sin to be sin for us, so that in him we might become the righteousness of God" (2 Cor. 5:21).

For Wesley, the sum and center of God's character, incarnate in Jesus of Nazareth, is the kind of generative *agapē* love that is the total antithesis of genocidal violence of any sort. It is a love that sees every person as a chosen being, fashioned in God's own image and imbued with his life-giving Spirit. It is a love that sees people as worthy of the supreme act of divine self-giving, even God's "one and only Son" (John 3:16). The sanctity of human life, established in creation, reaffirmed after the Flood, and codified in the sixth commandment, reaches its highest expression and ultimate affirmation in the Incarnation. Alice McDermott rightly points out that "the incredible notion of God made flesh . . . changing forever the fate of humankind . . . cannot logically be sustained, if any single life [is] expendable. . . . If any one life can be dismissed as meaningless, so too can the life of Christ."[52]

Elie Wiesel records a poignant scene that occurred when he and hundreds of other Jews were barracked for three days at Gleiwitz, Poland. They were pressed into a room so tightly that many were smothered by the sheer mass of human bodies cutting off sources of air. Twisted among the bodies was an emaciated young Warsaw Jew named Juliek. Somehow, incredibly, Juliek had clutched his violin during the forced march through snowstorms to Gleiwitz. That night, crammed among the hundreds of dead and nearly suffocating humans, Juliek struggled free and began to play a fragment from Beethoven's concerto. The sounds were pure, eerie, out of place in such a setting. Wiesel recalls:

> It was pitch dark. I could hear only the violin, and it was as though Juliek's soul were the bow. He was playing his life. The whole of his life was gliding on the strings—his lost hopes, his charred past, his extinguished future. He played as he would never play again.
>
> I shall never forget Juliek. How could I forget that concert, given to an audience of dying and dead men! To

[52]Alice McDermott, "Confessions of a Reluctant Catholic," in *The Best Christian Writing, 2001*, ed. John Wilson (San Francisco: HarperCollins, 2001), 201.

[53]Wiesel, *Night*, 107–8.

this day, whenever I hear Beethoven played my eyes close and out of the dark rises the sad, pale face of my Polish friend, as he said farewell on his violin to an audience of dying men.

I do not know for how long he played. I was overcome by sleep. When I awoke, in the daylight, I could see Juliek, opposite me, slumped over, dead. Near him lay his violin, smashed, trampled, a strange overwhelming little corpse.[53]

Where was God in Israel's genocidal conquest of Canaan? In the "lost hopes," the "charred past," the "extinguished future" of the babies, the infants, the little children—all the "Julieks" of Canaan. It was in those like Melchizedek, "priest of God Most High" (Gen. 14:18), and Rahab, who might have glorified God had they been given the chance.

RESPONSES TO
C. S. COWLES

A RESPONSE TO C. S. COWLES

Eugene H. Merrill

I begin by commending Professor Cowles for the clear, articulate, and reasoned way he has presented his point of view. Given his premises, he has constructed an argument that confronts all the issues with disarming persuasiveness. But it is precisely at the point of these premises that his case founders and, in fact, raises considerable concern. His approach can be gathered around four fundamental issues or tensions, all of them characterized by the term in his title, *radical discontinuity*. These are (1) the opposition of the New Testament to the Old Testament, (2) the difference between the God of the New Testament and the God of the Old Testament, (3) his Christocentric hermeneutics, and (4) the Old Testament as abiding revelation.

The New Testament versus the Old Testament. Though Cowles admits that the Old Testament is Christian Scripture, he makes the astounding assertion that "its message is not of and by itself a Christian message" (quoting John Bright's *The Authority of Scripture*). With this comment he opens the door to what can, in effect, be construed as a decanonizing of three-fourths of the Bible.

In particular, Cowles speaks of "divinely initiated and sanctioned violence" as a prime example of radical discontinuity between the Testaments. He correctly points out that there is, indeed, a certain degree of supersessionism apparent in the transition between the old and new covenants, one attested to by the New Testament itself (e.g., Matt. 7:12; John 1:17; Heb. 1:4–14). He pushes the matter too far, however, when, for example, he interprets Jesus' instruction to Peter to put away his sword (Matt. 26:52; Luke 22:51) as directly countermanding Moses in "forbidding the use of violence of any sort." Surely Jesus is not thinking of ḥerem or holy war in this setting, nor is he using the incident as a way of rebutting the Old Testament use of violence. He is merely making the point that he is resigned to the will of the Father and that no steps ought to be taken to subvert that will.[1] In the final analysis, for Cowles only what Jesus endorsed in the Old Testament can continue to be the Word of God for the church. The implications of this view of the relationship of the Old and New Testaments receives further treatment below.

The God of the New Testament versus the God of the Old Testament. To put the matter this way is to speak in rather Bultmannian terms, but Cowles promotes this kind of bifurcation by his question: "How do we harmonize the warrior God of Israel with the God of love incarnate in Jesus?" That this is not merely a rhetorical device to generate deep thinking on the matter is clear from his ensuing discussion. He argues that "insuperable difficulties for Christian theology, ethics, and praxis" arise when one attempts to attribute such atrocities as holy war "to the actual intention and will of God." As we will see, Cowles attempts to resolve this dilemma by suggesting that God had, indeed, never authorized such a policy but was only mistakenly thought to have done so. But this raises serious questions about the credibility of the Old Testament witness.

Quoting Walter Wink's *Engaging the Powers*, Cowles suggests that "against such an image of God [as warrior] the revolt of atheism is an act of pure religion." He continues in his own words: "To attribute genocidal violence to God poisons the well of all his other attributes." One must conclude either that the Old Testament God is a brute or that those who wrote of him in the sacred text totally misunderstood him. Cowles clearly rejects the former option but is left with one hardly better. If indeed the God of Israel appears to be a heartless and bloody tyrant for having authorized genocide, then that is what he must be if the Old Testament is to be understood by normal exegesis. But if there is another way to understand holy war besides viewing it as Cowles does, such distasteful ways of describing God have no value; indeed, they are to be abhorred.

---

[1]Darrell L. Bock, *Luke*, 2 vols. (Grand Rapids: Baker, 1996), 2:1771.

The distinction between the "two gods" appears also in Cowles's assertion that "God is not like the first Joshua, a warrior, but like the second, the Prince of Peace." Not only does this claim ignore texts that portray Yahweh as warrior (e.g., Ex. 15:3), but it overlooks eschatological descriptions of this same Prince of Peace as one who "judges and makes war," who is "dressed in a robe dipped in blood," and from whose mouth "comes a sharp sword with which to strike down the nations" (Rev. 19:11–15).

Even stronger is his admonition that Christians should not view God as the "God of Abraham, the God of Isaac and the God of Jacob" (Ex. 3:6) but as the "Father of our Lord Jesus Christ, the Father of compassion and the God of all comfort" (2 Cor. 1:3). But Jesus himself cited the same Old Testament text to define God as "not the God of the dead but of the living" (Matt. 22:32). Peter made the connection even more clearly: "The God of Abraham, Isaac and Jacob, the God of our fathers, has glorified his servant Jesus" (Acts 3:13; cf. 7:32). Neither Jesus nor Peter is willing to admit to any distinction between the God of Israel and the God of the church.

In line with his Christocentric hermeneutics, Cowles views the God of the Old Testament as one who must be understood in the light of Jesus and concludes that "the God revealed in Jesus never has been and never will be party to genocide of any sort, for 'God is love' (1 John 4:8)." Such a reading either permits the existence of two Gods or requires a massive rereading of Old Testament texts that explicitly attribute genocide to God (e.g., Num. 21:2; Deut. 2:34; 3:6; 7:2; 13:15; Josh. 6:21). Anticipating the response that God judges sin and sinners to destruction and death, he proposes an idea commonly espoused to deliver God from this onus, namely, that sin contains the seed of its own destruction so that God need not be charged with the suffering and death of sinners in hell. Violence and death "are the work of Satan." He concludes that "there is no support in the New [Testament] for imaging God as one who wills the indiscriminate slaughter of human beings." This, of course, ignores eschatological passages and tacitly relegates the Old Testament to subcanonical authority.

Christocentric hermeneutics. Throughout his paper, Cowles insists that Christ be the hermeneutical and theological lens through which the Old Testament must be read. In a clear and telling statement he suggests that "in the New Testament, Jesus is not defined by God; rather, God is defined by Jesus." While there is some measure of truth in this by itself, he goes on to argue that Jesus reinterpreted the Old Testament God and his ways by "editing out" troublesome allusions to God's wrathful side. He cites, for example, Jesus' Nazareth sermon, in which he eliminated the "prophetic punch line" that speaks of the "day of vengeance of our God" (Isa. 61:1–2; cf. Luke 4:18–19). This was done, however, not because Jesus wished to downplay this fearful side of God's nature but because he was inaugurating the day of good news and not bad news.[2] Jesus did not shirk to speak of judgment when the setting was more appropriate (e.g., Matt. 10:15; 11:22–24; John 5:22; 2 Cor. 5:10; Rev. 14:7).

On a broader scale, Cowles proposes that "if we take love as it is revealed by God in Christ as our criterion for interpreting Scripture, then the 'tension between texts' [of the Old and New Testaments] can be transcended." In effect, ordinary historical-grammatical exegesis of the Old Testament must be suspended where offensive texts are concerned. If they fall short of our perception as to God's love, they must be radically reinterpreted. Such subjectivism of method is most disquieting and dangerous.

Even more disturbing is the claim that "while Jesus affirmed the Hebrew Scriptures as the authentic Word of God, he did not endorse every word in them as God's." The inference is crystal clear—some parts of the Old Testament are the words of humans and some the words of God. Presumably each interpreter must decide for himself or herself which is which. But precisely such hermeneutics are necessary if one is to discount "genocide" texts, for example, as having revelatory value. Followed logically, one can eviscerate the Old Testament of any apparently "sub-Christian" ethic. This, in fact, is what Cowles is prepared to do when he argues that Jesus' command to "love your enemies" (Matt. 5:44) "represents a total repudiation of Moses' [sic!] genocidal commands and stands in judgment on Joshua's campaign of ethnic cleansing." If the words of Moses were indeed only the words of Moses, they might well stand condemned. But when the record states, "The LORD said to Moses . . . 'Do to [Og] what you did to Sihon [i.e., he annihilated

---

[2]Robert H. Stein, *Luke* (NAC 24; Nashville: Broadman, 1992), 157.

him]'" (Num. 31:34), God himself must be charged with the inflammatory accusation of "ethnic cleansing."

To speak, then, of Christocentric hermeneutics is to use language out of keeping with Jesus' own understanding and use of the Old Testament. Furthermore, if Jesus is the criterion by which the authority of the Bible and its meaning are to be judged, to what extent can we be confident that that same Bible is a faithful witness to what our Lord said and did? To say that only the New Testament provides a reliable witness is to beg the question and to relegate the Old Testament to a Marcion-like obsolescence.

The Old Testament as abiding revelation. We have already noted the lines of demarcation drawn by Cowles between the Old Testament and the New and between the God of the Old Testament and the God of the New. That, with his Christocentric hermeneutics, casts doubt on the Old Testament as revelation—or at least nuances that term in alarmingly misleading ways. The following few citations make this abundantly clear.

First, Cowles, speaking of an Old Testament history "saturated with violence," proposes that it was *"believed* to be divinely initiated and sanctioned" (emphasis added). One must conclude that it really was not at all and that such impetus came from human origin. Then, as though that might be too jarring a concept, he resorts to a method of exegesis practiced throughout the history of the church in dealing with such difficulties, namely, to assume that the writers of the sacred texts were employing figurative language such as allegory. Quoting Duane Christensen's commentary on Deuteronomy, Cowles views Joshua's holy-war exploits as "a metaphor of spiritual warfare." That is, there never was such a historical encounter nor did God intend for there to be. The abuse of unsubstantiated allegory is well known in the history of interpretation. Appeal to it here is a throwback to a mode of exegesis abandoned by most modern scholars.

Second, Cowles proposes that another way out of the dilemma is to grasp the principle of "the progressive *understanding* of God's self-disclosure" (emphasis his). By this he expressly does not mean progressive revelation. Rather, according to Cowles, as Old Testament thinkers succeeded each other over the centuries, they came to see how wrong their forebears had been and therefore saw the need to correct them by more palatable belief and praxis.

Cowles cites as an example 2 Samuel 24:1, which states that God led David to take his ill-conceived census of Israel, and the much later rendition of this episode in 1 Chronicles 21:1, which attributes the sinful act to Satan. The Old Testament thus becomes self-corrective until it reaches its moral and theological perfection in the New Testament. Yet one should not be harsh toward the Old Testament writers, suggests Cowles, for they "were telling the truth as they understood it." In reference to God's annihilation of the Canaanites, God alone had to bear the onus for it in the early Old Testament literature because, according to Cowles, "the Israelites had no concept of Satan prior to the Babylonian exile."

As this analysis demonstrates, Professor Cowles's case for radical discontinuity is sustained not by a sensitive recognition of the principle of progressive revelation, which allows differences between Old Testament and New Testament viewpoints on issues such as genocide, but by driving a wedge between the Testaments that effectively denies that the God of Israel is the God of the church or, at the very least, devalues the Old Testament as an authentic revelation of the character and purposes of God. Such a solution is unlikely to be persuasive, at least to those who hold the Bible in its entirety to be a sure word from God.

A RESPONSE TO C. S. COWLES

Daniel L. Gard

If, as becomes apparent in my other two responses, I find myself in "spiritual continuity" with Tremper Longman and "moderate discontinuity" with Eugene Merrill, I am most certainly in "radical discontinuity" with C. S. Cowles. In spite of major disagreements with Cowles, I must say that I find his approach to be refreshing and honest insofar as he sets forth his position with unusual clarity. Unfortunately, the position he takes does not take us to a perspective on God and the Scriptures that truly responds to the ethical question evoked by the Old Testament texts.

Cowles asserts that "if we take love as it is revealed by God in Christ as our criterion for interpreting Scripture, then the 'tension between texts' can be transcended." I certainly agree that Christ is the key to interpreting the Bible, both Old and New Testaments. Yet I cannot agree that "tension between texts" can readily be transcended. There are several reasons for this.

(1) Either "all Scripture is God-breathed and is useful for teaching, rebuking, correcting and training in righteousness" (2 Tim. 3:16), or it is not. This is a fundamental hermeneutical stance that shapes the way in which one understands any biblical text, including those that make us the most uncomfortable. Cowles himself cites the words of Jesus in Matthew 5:17, "Do not think that I have come to abolish the Law or the Prophets; I have not come to abolish them but to fulfill them." Although Cowles correctly points out that Jesus frequently uses the formula "You have heard it said.... But I tell you..." and "that his

way of fulfilling them was to recast them according to the law of love," this in no way repudiates the Old Testament Scripture. What is written is written, and it is either truthful or false. Jesus deals with the Scriptures in such a way that he does not contradict them but explains them according to the meaning he originally intended them to have.

(2) Cowles radically reduces the Old Testament to literature that can and must have value according to whatever standards we choose to impose. On this Cowles is clear: "If we believe that Jesus is truly 'the image of the invisible God' (Col. 1:15), then we must resist all efforts to defend Old Testament genocidal commands as reflective of the will and character of God. Since Jesus has come, we are under no obligation to justify that which cannot be justified but can only be described as *pre-Christ, sub-Christ, and anti-Christ*" (emphasis added). In this case, Jesus himself was wrong when he insisted that the Scriptures (i.e., the Old Testament) spoke of him.

If the methodology of Cowles is consistently followed, then Scripture becomes merely a piece of modeling clay that can be formed and manipulated into whatever the reader chooses to make it. Nothing is certain about God, the incarnation of the Son, or the salvation of the human race.

(3) Cowles seems to view the Old Testament as simply a collection of religious writings that reflect the way in which religious thinkers understood God at certain points in Israel's history. I do not at all agree, for example, that "the Israelites had no concept of Satan prior to the Babylonian exile." Already in Genesis 3 we find a reference to a personal evil being, whom later writers call Satan (cf. Job 1–2). In his discussion of 2 Samuel 24 and 1 Chronicles 21, Cowles correctly notes that the Chronicler attributes the census of Israel to Satan's inciting of David rather than to Yahweh's inciting of David. But to use this as Cowles does completely misunderstands the nature of the Chronicler's work. Through his work, the Chronicler provides a theological interpretation of Israel's history based on the text of Samuel–Kings. The Chronicler understands Yahweh as the Lord of history who uses all things to accomplish his divine purposes. Even Satan is subject to God's power and became the instrument of Yahweh in bringing about the census.

For some, this interpretation of the Chronicler's history may not be satisfying but rather will be seen as further evidence of the humanness of the biblical record. This is again a matter of presupposition. With all of its human authors (whether Moses, the Chronicler, or Paul), is the Bible inspired by God so that its words are in fact the words of God? I affirm that it is. Thus, I must fundamentally reject not only Cowles's interpretation of Chronicles but also his repeated assertion that certain texts reflect the opinion of a human such as Moses and that those texts are negated by the word of God spoken by Jesus. In my view, the word of Moses is as much the word of God as the recorded word of Jesus. One does not trump the other.

(4) Finally, where does Cowles take us in our thinking about God? He raises the important point of van de Beek's description of God, that "good and evil both come forth from his will." Cowles rightly questions van de Beek but offers a solution to the problem that I find less than helpful.

Like Cowles, I reject van de Beek's notion that both good and evil come from the will of God. Nothing evil can be attributed to God because God is in his very essence good. Evil is attributable only to humanity in its fallen state and the concomitant rebellion of this creation against its good and gracious Creator. Even Christians, who have been restored to a relationship of peace with God through Christ, live with the effects of sin. Our bodies age and suffer, we live with the results of sin all around us, we fail miserably to keep the Lord's statutes and commandments—and our minds are incapable of even comprehending the ultimate "good." We cannot set ourselves up as judges of what God has said and done as if we, in our limitations, had the insight and wisdom to judge God's actions.

For this reason, we may not marginalize any text of Scripture, including the very ones that present insurmountable intellectual issues to us. We cannot pick and choose which biblical texts we can accept as coming from God and reflect his will and word. What appears to the human mind as "evil" acts of God (such as the genocide commands against the Canaanites) are in fact not "evil" acts at all since they come from the Lord himself. There simply comes a point in which human reason must bow to the divine and recognize that his ways are truly not ours and his thoughts are truly above our own (cf. Isa. 55:8–9).

I do appreciate Cowles's treatment of the incarnate Son as One whose words bring good things into this world of darkness, war, and death. I must raise the issue, however, of whether the New Testament eschatological texts regarding Jesus do not shatter Cowles's radical split between God in the Old Testament and in the New Testament. It is true that Jesus did not come as a warrior. His earthly ministry did not involve any implementation of destruction on anyone who threatened him. Even on the cross he prayed for those who crucified him. In his face, one sees the face of God turned toward this fallen world with hope and life and forgiveness.

Still, other pages of the New Testament present the same Jesus as One who returns not in poverty and humility but in glory and power. He does not return as One who brings the way of salvation. Rather, he returns as the righteous Judge who speaks the final word of judgment on the living and the dead— and a fierce judgment it is for those who face it apart from him. The final judgment with its utter destruction of the heavens and the earth and all those at enmity with God makes the most bloody warfare narratives of the Old Testament seem like children's bedtime stories. And this comes from the same Jesus who then and now speaks words of peace and invitation during this time of salvation. On the Judgment Day, however, that invitation ends, and destruction unlike anything the universe has ever seen will occur.

God in the Old Testament is precisely the same God in the New Testament. He has revealed himself through the prophets and apostles and most especially in the life, death, and resurrection of his Son Jesus. At all times from Adam to the Last Day, he has reached out to this world with grace and mercy. That some, whether ancient Canaanites or children of Adam yet to be born, reject his grace and thus face the divine *herem* does not contradict the love that is God's essence. It rather calls us to marvel at his wonderful grace toward us who believe and to acknowledge that all his ways and thoughts are above our own.

Although I have been critical of C. S. Cowles's position, as a final comment I do wish to thank him for the honest and clear explication of his position. He has challenged unreflected thinking that can lead to usurpation of divine prerogatives by human beings who seek to impose their own *herem* on others.

A RESPONSE TO C. S. COWLES

Tremper Longman III

Dr. Cowles has written a clear and strongly argued essay in support of the perspective of radical discontinuity. He interprets well those Scripture passages that he finds conducive to his approach, and he writes with a passion that is in keeping with the subject and that shows his love of Christ and God's human creatures.

There are important areas in which I find myself in significant agreement with his argument, and these areas of agreement may be seen by comparing his essay with mine. In the first place, I strongly believe as he does that Jesus Christ is the center of scriptural revelation. As Augustine pointed out, "the New Testament is in the Old concealed, and the Old is in the New revealed." Luke 24:25–27, 44–48, which Cowles cites, is determinative of this, where Jesus himself affirms that the entirety of the Old Testament anticipates his coming suffering and glorification. In this Cowles and I agree on a matter that places us in the minority of even evangelical interpreters. Most biblical scholars today want to argue that it is wrong to read the Old Testament in the light of the New Testament. They feel that it distorts the unique witness of the Old Testament. On the contrary, Cowles and I think it is critically important for Christians ultimately to read the Old in the light of the surprising ending in Christ.[1]

In spite of this agreement in principle, however, it quickly becomes obvious that we disagree over the significance of this

---

[1]See my *Reading the Bible with Heart and Mind* (Colorado Springs: NavPress, 1997).

truth for our reading and appreciation of the Old Testament. But before developing our disagreement any further, let me point out one other similarity. Cowles and I are in total agreement concerning the fact that Old Testament holy-war texts provide absolutely no justification for the present-day Christian to engage in warfare or violence of any kind. Again, we arrive at this position in somewhat different ways (see my essay for details of my argument), but still this is a substantial agreement.[2] Christians should never take up arms in the name of Christ.

Where we disagree, and here disagree passionately, is in our view of canon. To reach the position that he takes up, Cowles in effect rejects the Old Testament as authoritative. In essence, in his argument Christ trumps the Old Testament. As he sees it, we are to read the Old Testament through the prism provided by Christ, and if there is disparity between the two, then the Old Testament is not authoritative.

That there is a radical transformation that takes place in Christ is absolutely true, so I can agree with quotes like the one he takes from Brueggemann to the effect that "Old Testament theological articulation does not conform to established church faith."[3] But he makes comments that go well beyond this. For instance, in his interaction with the Reformed theologian A. van de Beek, he disparagingly describes him as taking "the received text of both Old and New Testaments as representing the literal words of God … [i]n that all parts of the Bible have equal weight of revelatory value." He goes on to insist that van de Beek must, therefore, portray God as "evil."

However, van de Beek would never say God is evil. True, he says that God may be cruel *in our eyes* and evil *in our eyes*—but that is precisely the point. Human perception is distorted and wrong. Van de Beek would affirm, however, that God by definition is good and that his actions by definition are good. God, not humans, defines what is good. There is no independent perspective by which we can hold judgment over God. Cowles at this point would disagree and say, "It's Jesus," and I would agree. But below we will see that in actuality the revela-

---

[2]Though in my case this does not lead me to a pacifist position, since I think that there are other biblical arguments in favor of just war, specifically one built on the doctrine of self-defense.

[3]Quoted from Walter Brueggemann, *Theology of the Old Testament* (Minneapolis: Fortress, 1997), 107.

tion of Jesus in the New Testament is no less violent than the revelation of God in the Old Testament. In other words, the divide that Cowles draws between Christ and the Old Testament is a false one. There is no discontinuity between the Testaments on this point.

Before dealing with this issue, though, perhaps I should emphasize my point that Cowles does denigrate the authority of the Old Testament. His low view of the Old Testament is implied in statements such as "the most incisive critique of God as destroyer occurs in the context of Jesus' final journey to Jerusalem." It is also implied in his comments about the injustice of God's ordering the destruction of the Canaanites, not to speak of his apparent agreement with Wesley and Wink that "Moses' genocidal commands [which, according to the text, are ultimately God's commands] make a mockery of God's justice, not to mention his holiness and love."

Against Cowles's view, I would point out that the Old Testament does not simply provide descriptions of God as destroyer but pictures God as commanding the destruction and prodding the Israelites into doing it. When they do not do it, the Old Testament describes God as punishing Israel. To say that the New Testament critiques this picture of God in the Old Testament is in effect to say that the Old Testament is not Scripture. His view pits Scripture against Scripture.

However, to be fair, it is true that Cowles does not quite come out and say that the Old Testament is not Scripture. He argues that the New Testament transforms the old wineskins of the Old Testament into new wineskins. He does not explicitly adopt a Marcionite position of Scripture, but the implications of many of his comments suggest such a position.

In a sense, I see Cowles taking the easy way out by adopting a view that simply rejects the idea of the "inerrancy and infallibility of all Scripture" and chooses those passages that he finds acceptable according to his view of Jesus. Here, then, is my final point: The picture of Jesus that Cowles gives us, through which he views and judges the Old Testament, is a selective one. It seems telling to me that Cowles avoids the judgment and divine warrior passages of the book of Revelation or any of the New Testament apocalyptic passages. One is led to ask why. After all, when the topic is God and violence, the apocalyptic texts are obviously relevant. Cowles never addresses Revelation head-on, nor does he explain to us why he does not address such a relevant and large part of the New Testament.

Thus, we are left to speculate. However, it seems obvious from what he has written that he would find these passages, at least as traditionally interpreted, to be just as unacceptable to his view of God as the Old Testament holy-war passages. As I point out in my essay, the New Testament, when taken as a whole, is just as violent and bloody as—actually, probably more than—the Old Testament.[4]

I do not know Cowles except through this essay, but he has given the impression there that he does not accept the whole of the Bible, the Bible by the way that Jesus himself clearly accepted in its entirety,[5] as authoritative. My hope is that in his passion for his position, he has stated things so strongly that I do not understand his position correctly. However, I have gone over his essay a number of times and am left with the above impression.

As I have tried to suggest in my essay, Cowles's way of denigrating the Old Testament is not the only way to deal with the obvious fact that in Jesus there is a radical transformation, intensification, and progression of revelation.

---

[4]Cowles also makes the curious comment that "it is surely a fact of inexhaustible significance that Jesus never used his supernatural miracle-working power to hurt, maim, coerce, conquer, or destroy." Perhaps not, but he used his human strength to flog the moneychangers out of the temple—or perhaps Cowles thinks this was just a threat. Even so, it was a threat of significant violence.

[5]For Jesus' view of the canon, see R. Beckwith, *The Old Testament Canon in the New Testament Church* (London: SPCK, 1985). Cowles's comment that "While Jesus affirmed the Hebrew Scriptures as the authentic Word of God, he did not endorse every word in them as God's" is baffling to me. What is the Word of God but God's words?

Chapter Two

THE CASE FOR MODERATE DISCONTINUITY

Eugene H. Merrill

THE CASE FOR
MODERATE DISCONTINUITY

Eugene H. Merrill

One of the most disturbing indices of the human condition is the fact that historians commonly recount the past in terms of conflict.[1] The historical record is periodized by this war or that, times of intervening peace appearing almost to be incidental to the metanarrative. This is true not only because war has such horrendous consequences but because by its very nature it holds a certain gruesome fascination to the human psyche. People are at once attracted and repelled by the fact of war, as the popular media can well attest. Among the best-sellers in print and the blockbusters of Hollywood are graphic re-creations of the bloody and destructive carnage of hostility, whether on the personal or international level.

The destruction of the World Trade Center on September 11, 2001, raised the level of the consciousness of the American people about the reality of war and its aftermath perhaps more than anything since Pearl Harbor, Normandy, and Hiroshima. The images of hijacked airliners plowing into those lofty towers, people leaping to their deaths to escape incineration, and the shuddering collapse of a million tons of wood, stone, and steel have been indelibly ingrained into the very fiber of the American people. Beyond this are the questions: How could this have happened? Who was responsible? How can they be found and punished? And most perplexing and poignant of all, where was God, and why did he allow this to happen?

---

[1]Peter C. Craigie, *The Problem of War in the Old Testament* (Grand Rapids: Eerdmans, 1978), 9.

Those inclined to think theistically found themselves wondering how a God of love could permit or perhaps even sanction such a cruel and devastating turn of events. These were, after all, innocent men, women, and children—both the living and the dead—who did nothing more than show up for work that day or bid good-bye to those who did. Was it random, was it arbitrary, or was it perhaps part of some grand but inscrutable plan of an all-knowing and all-powerful God who in this act displayed facets of his character and person other than those more commonly associated with him: grace, mercy, and compassion?

Readers of the Old Testament who think long and hard about God's dealings with individuals and nations in ancient times have already raised these questions and more, for the narrative from Adam to the Chronicler is blood-soaked with murder and war.[2] Indeed, these issues are addressed in the sacred annals themselves, particularly in the poetic and wisdom texts. Over and over Israel's thinkers ponder the ways of God and strive without success to accommodate their understanding of a beneficent God to the reality of everyday life with its experiences of disease, pain, war, and death. Theodicy, a major theological motif in these writings, addresses head-on the apparently irreconcilable polarities of God's tender love and terrible wrath. Put popularly the question is: Why do the righteous suffer? Put more theologically it is: How can the ways of God be explained to human understanding and satisfaction, if at all?[3]

Nowhere in the modern reading of Old Testament texts is the theodicic problem more acute than in coming to grips with so-called "holy war," more commonly and correctly described now as "Yahweh war."[4] Common in this concept was genocide,

---

[2]Ben C. Ollenburger, "Introduction," in Gerhard von Rad, *Holy War in Ancient Israel*, ed. and trans. Marva J. Dawn (Grand Rapids: Eerdmans, 1991), 3, citing Wellhausen's observations on the matter.

[3]Walter Brueggemann, *Theology of the Old Testament* (Minneapolis: Fortress, 1997), 385–99. Dhorme says of Job that the "contrast between his expectation (29:18–20) and the sad reality (30:1ff.) is a flat contradiction to the whole system of morals based on the equation of moral good and material happiness" (E. Dhorme, *A Commentary on the Book of Job*, trans. Harold Knight [Nashville: Thomas Nelson, 1984], cxliii).

[4]Rudolf Smend, *Yahweh War and Tribal Confederation*, trans. Max Gray Rogers (Nashville: Abingdon, 1970), 38; G. H. Jones, "The Concept of Holy War," in *The World of Ancient Israel*, ed. R. E. Clements (Cambridge: Cambridge Univ. Press, 1989), 313–14; J. P. U. Lilley, "Understanding the Ḥerem," *TynBul* 44 (1993): 173.

the wholesale slaughter of men, women, and children. Usually carried out against the Canaanites and other indigenous Palestinian peoples, on rare occasions Israelites themselves could be targeted.

God initiated the process by singling out those destined to destruction, empowering an agent (usually his chosen people Israel) to accomplish it, and guaranteeing its successful conclusion once the proper conditions were met. The purpose of this study is to identify Yahweh war as distinct from war in general, to determine its characteristic features, to attempt to justify it in light of the character of God as a whole, and to determine to what extent such a notion is continuous or discontinuous with the New Testament and applicable to modern life.

RELEVANT OLD TESTAMENT PASSAGES

A proper investigation of the issues just raised requires attention to the biblical texts that specifically speak to them. These are both prescriptive (primarily in Torah, i.e., legal texts) and descriptive (primarily in the historical narratives). That is, they regulate the practice of Yahweh war and then provide accounts of how such war was actually carried out. The approach to be followed will be (1) to provide a brief overview of battle accounts in general, especially those that appear to have overtones of Yahweh war;[5] (2) to isolate those that incorporate undeniable traits of genocide, including the use of technical terms such as *ḥrm/ḥerem*; and (3) to reexamine these latter accounts from a theological and ethical point of view in an attempt to understand their contribution to an overall biblical theodicy.

The Legislation of Yahweh War

Though hints of the rationale for Yahweh war and its prosecution occur prior to the revelation of the covenant at Sinai (cf.

---

[5]My student Milad Dagher, in an unpublished paper, has identified at least fifty-nine battle accounts from the event of the Exodus to the Babylonian destruction of Jerusalem. About one-fourth of these contain clear references to Yahweh war. Lind lists eleven of the "more dramatic episodes" in which the theology of Yahweh war is dominant (Millard Lind, "Paradigm of Holy War in the Old Testament," *BR* 16 [1971]: 30).

Ex. 3:8–12, 17–20; 4:22–23; 6:6–8; 7:3–5, 17–18; 9:13–17; 11:4–8; 12:12, 29–33; 13:14–16; 14:10–25; 15:1–18, 21; 17:8–16), it was only after Israel had been constituted as a nation following that revelation that Yahweh war became not just a display of God's redemptive power and grace on behalf of his people but a constituent part of the covenant relationship itself.[6] Israel from then on would not just witness God's mighty deeds as heavenly warrior but would be engaged in bringing them to pass.

The first articulation of Yahweh war appears at the end of the so-called "Book of the Covenant" (Ex. 23:20–33),[7] a section that, with 20:22–23, forms an inclusio bracketing the whole covenant text.[8] The common theme of the two passages is the need to recognize that only Yahweh is God and only he is to be worshiped. In addition to this declaration, 23:20–33 spells out the need to destroy the nations of Canaan for they are the enemies of Yahweh as well as of Israel (23:22–23, 27–30); the reason they are enemies is because they worship and serve other gods.[9] They must be destroyed, then, lest Israel follow after these gods, thus violating the first two commandments of the Decalogue (23:24–25; cf. 20:3–5).

Other glimpses of Yahweh war may be found in Leviticus 26:3–45; Numbers 14:39–45; 21:1–3; and 31:1–20, but not in complete and sustained form. It is in connection with covenant renewal in Moab that Yahweh war reaches its definitive expression, particularly in Deuteronomy 20:1–20. In this manual of war, principles are established for the conduct of war in general (20:1–15) and Yahweh war in particular (20:16–20). In each case

---

[6]Ollenburger, "Introduction," 4–5; Millard Lind, *Yahweh Is a Warrior* (Scottdale, Pa.: Herald, 1980), 148–49; Joel S. Kaminsky, "Joshua 7: A Reassessment of Israelite Conceptions of Corporate Punishment," in *The Pitcher Is Broken: Memorial Essays for Gösta W. Ahlström*, ed. Steven W. Holloway and Lowell K. Handy (JSOTSup 190; Sheffield: Sheffield Academic Press, 1995), 343; Reuven Firestone, "Conceptions of Holy War in Biblical and Qur'anic Tradition," *JRE* 24 (1996): 105; Michael Walzer, "The Idea of Holy War in Ancient Israel," *JRE* 20 (1992): 216.

[7]Lilley, "Understanding the Ḥerem," 174.

[8]John I. Durham, *Exodus* (WBC 13; Waco, Tex.: Word, 1987), 334.

[9]Philip D. Stern, *The Biblical Ḥerem: A Window on Israel's Religious Experience* (BJS 211; Atlanta: Scholars Press, 1991), 104, 110, 123; Richard D. Nelson, "Ḥerem and the Deuteronomic Social Conscience," in *Deuteronomy and Deuteronomic Literature: Festschrift C. H. W. Brekelmans*, ed. M. Vervenne and J. Lust (BETL 133; Leuven: Peeters/Leuven Univ. Press, 1997), 53.

Yahweh is present, and there are elements common to both to suggest that the conflicts in view are not in any way secular. This chapter will come in for detailed treatment at a later point.

The vantage point of Deuteronomy is the impending conquest of Canaan in fulfillment of the promises to the patriarchs. It is clear that the land was considered Israel's by divine right and that the nations who occupied it were little better than squatters. Yahweh, as owner of the land, would therefore undertake measures to destroy and/or expel the illegitimate inhabitants, and he would do so largely through his people Israel and by means of Yahweh war. A number of passages either mandate this approach (Deut. 7:1–5, 17–26; 9:1–5; 12:1–3; 13:12–18; 20:16–20) or present it as already having taken place in the Transjordan (2:30–37; 3:1–3).

The Narratives of Yahweh War

While for the most part described in the post-Mosaic era, there are narrative descriptions of Yahweh war in the Torah. The earliest is the Exodus account, where Yahweh led the hosts of Israel (Ex. 13:21–22), fought for them (14:14), divided the sea (14:21–22), drowned the Egyptian army (14:26–28), and proved by all this that he is Lord (14:31). In the poetic account he is called a "warrior" (15:3; lit., "man of war"), the incomparable One among all the gods (15:11). His conquest of Egypt betokens his everlasting sovereignty (15:18).[10]

The ill-fated attempt by Israel to enter Canaan prematurely (Num. 14:39–45) was followed up later by a defensive conflict in which Yahweh led his armies in triumph over the Canaanites of Arad (21:1–3). Shortly thereafter the Amorites under King Sihon fell to Israel (21:21–30), a campaign described in Deuteronomy 2:26–37 as Yahweh war. The same is true of the defeat of King Og of Bashan (Num. 21:31–35; cf. Deut. 3:1–17). The retaliatory battle against Midian (Num. 31:1–24) is also clearly Yahweh war, though the technical language is largely missing.

The conquest of Canaan obviously involved Yahweh war since that was in line with the Deuteronomic mandate. Jericho was taken and destroyed in this manner (Josh. 6), as was the fortified city of Ai (8:24–29). There are overtones of Yahweh war

---

[10]Lind, *Yahweh Is a Warrior*, 46–54.

in the defeat of the Amorite coalition (10:5–14) and in the summary of Joshua's entire southern campaign, in which Yahweh took the initiative in the defeat of Hazor and its allies (11:1–15). In fact, the entire conquest is attributed to divine initiative and intervention (11:16–20).

The book of Judges attests to the fact of Yahweh war, sometimes with only brief allusion to technical terms (1:17, 18–19, 22–26; 3:7–11, 12–30, 31) and sometimes with more overt and lengthy descriptions. Note, for example, that the Song of Deborah declares that Yahweh marched forth from Edom (5:4), came down to join Deborah in battle (5:13), and marshaled the very hosts of heaven against Sisera and the Canaanites (5:19–21).[11] The narrator also makes clear that Gideon's success in destroying the Midianites was attributable to the aid of Yahweh (cf. 6:11–12; 7:9, 14).

Under Samuel, Yahweh achieved great victory over the Philistines (1 Sam. 7:5–14). After fasting and confession the people called on Yahweh for salvation (7:6, 9), a prayer God answered with decisiveness (7:10). The place then received the name Ebenezer ("stone of help") to commemorate Yahweh's leadership in delivering the nation (7:12). King Saul also knew something of Yahweh's presence and power in battle (11:6–7), and he misguidedly attempted to appropriate the protocols of Yahweh war by appealing to the ark or ephod with their priestly associations (14:18–19). His battle against the Amalekites is clearly one of Yahweh war despite his disobedience in carrying out fully the prophetic commission of God (15:3, 8, 15, 20). David's reign also provides a number of instances of Yahweh war, or at least war in which elements of Yahweh's intervention may be seen. The catalog of victories compiled in 2 Samuel 8 makes clear that success lay in divine initiative and intervention (8:6, 14).

The last example of Yahweh war is the marvelous deliverance of Jerusalem from Sennacherib of Assyria in the days of King Hezekiah (2 Kings 18:13–19:37).[12] After taunts and threats from the Assyrian spokesmen, Hezekiah repented, entered the

---

[11]P. D. Miller Jr., *The Divine Warrior in Early Israel* (HSM 5; Cambridge, Mass.: Harvard Univ. Press, 1973), 161–62; Moshe Weinfeld, "Divine Intervention in War in Ancient Israel and in the Ancient Near East," in *History, Historiography and Interpretation*, ed. H. Tadmor and M. Weinfeld (Jerusalem: Magnes, 1984), 124–31.

[12]Stern, *The Biblical Ḥerem*, 185; Lind, *Yahweh Is a Warrior*, 141.

temple, summoned Isaiah the prophet to intercede with Yahweh on his behalf, and confessed that Yahweh was sovereign and that his reputation was at stake. Isaiah responded that Yahweh would save the city and would do so for his own sake and for the sake of David, with whom he had made a solemn covenant. Following that was the elimination of the Assyrian army by the angel of Yahweh.

YAHWEH-WAR FORMULAS AND TEXTS

As with any institution or practice governed by conventional patterns, Yahweh-war passages have their own set of technical terms and unique form-critical characteristics. Most scholars agree that no one passage contains them all; in fact, few have even a majority of them. In his seminal study of 1951, Gerhard von Rad isolated the following elements as indicative of the presence of Yahweh-war ideology,[13] an analysis that continues to enjoy much favor:

(1) mustering by a trumpet call
(2) consecration of the men (Josh. 3:5)
(3) offering of sacrifices
(4) an oracle of God
(5) "Yahweh has given"
(6) Yahweh leads the way
(7) designated as "Yahweh war" (1 Sam. 18:17; 25:28)
(8) "fear not" formula
(9) enemy's loss of courage
(10) war cry (*teru'ah*)
(11) divine terror
(12) *herem* ("the high point")
(13) "to your tents" (1 Sam. 4:10)

It is obvious that the occurrence of *hrm/herem* is a striking feature of Yahweh war, a criterion accepted by nearly all scholars.[14] However, 2 Chronicles 20:1–30, one of the most famous examples

---

[13]Von Rad, *Holy War in Ancient Israel*, 41–51.

[14]Thus Jones, "The Concept of Holy War," 309; see Sa-Moon Kang, *Divine War in the Old Testament and in the Ancient Near East* (BZAW 177; Berlin: Walter de Gruyter, 1989), 142–43; N. K. Gottwald, "'Holy War' in Deuteronomy: Analysis and Critique," *RevExp* 61 (1964): 299.

of such a conflict, contains none of these terms though it does refer
to Levites in place of priests. Moreover, certain passages lacking
in most of the terms are nonetheless recognized as providing
paradigmatic insight into the nature and purpose of Yahweh war.
These include especially Deuteronomy 7:1–5 and 13:12–18, both of
which will be addressed at a later point. Our intent to limit Yahweh war to genocide precludes consideration of instances where
other, less-drastic forms of Yahweh war might occur.

Of all the terms to be considered, only *ḥrm/ḥerem* needs any
extensive study because of its indispensability in Yahweh-war
and genocide contexts. The root *ḥrm* in Hebrew has the idea of
both destruction and separation or devotion, both nuances
occurring together in some passages.[15] Its usage also depends
on its collocation with other terms and the synonyms and/or
antonyms with which it is associated.

The best approach to understanding the nature of Old Testament genocide, the ethics of its implementation, and its implications vis-à-vis the character of God is to look inductively at
the major texts that authorize and/or describe it and to draw
appropriate conclusions. This will begin with consideration of
the lexical and literary features of these passages, to be followed
in subsequent sections with the historical, cultural, and theological occasions for this kind of Yahweh war and the Old Testament justification for it.

Deuteronomy 20:1–20

Sometimes described as Israel's "Manual of War," this text
prescribes Israel's behavior with regard to the conquest of
Canaan that lay in the immediate future.[16] It is divided into two
parts: (1) instructions about "ordinary" war (Deut. 20:1–15) and
(2) instructions about Yahweh war (20:16–20). The focus here
will be on the latter, but there are clearly overtones of Yahweh
war in the whole passage. Among these are (1) the injunction
not to fear because of God's presence (20:1, 3–4); (2) the involvement of cultic personnel (20:2); (3) the assurance that Yahweh is
the warrior (20:4); (4) the certainty of the outcome (20:13); (5) the
slaughter of all the men (in the case of ordinary war, 20:13) or of

---

[15]N. Lohfink, "חָרַם," *TDOT*, 5:180–99; J. Naudé, "חרם," *NIDOTTE*, 2:276–77.
[16]Von Rad, *Holy War in Ancient Israel*, 115–16; Lind, *Yahweh Is a Warrior*, 134.

all others as well (in the case of Yahweh war, 20:16–17); (6) the taking of plunder (in ordinary war, 20:14); and (7) the reason for the total destruction (in Yahweh war, 20:18), that is, to preclude Israel's adoption of pagan ways. Technical terms found here include *ḥrm* (utter destruction, 20:17), *milḥamah* (war, 20:1), *kohen* (priest, 20:2), and *nkh* (smiting, 20:13), the first two of which occurs in the Yahweh-war section.

Deuteronomy 13:12–18

Deuteronomy 13:12–18 contains some of the common terms for Yahweh war, such as the utter destruction (*ḥrm*), smiting (*nkh*), and burning (*śrp*), but it is radically different in that this time Yahweh war is directed against persons and places in Israel itself.[17] The context is the possibility of apostasy within the covenant community and what is to be done to those who take the lead in it, especially false prophets (13:1–11), and the cities that harbor them. Such places are as guilty before God as any Canaanite city; thus, the judgment must be precisely the same— the application of Yahweh war. The punishment is smiting (*nkh*) with the sword, utter destruction (*ḥrm*) of goods and properties, and devotion of the city and its spoil to Yahweh by fire (*śrp*) (13:15–16a). The site must forever remain abandoned (13:16b), and nothing devoted (*herem*) can be appropriated for personal use (cf. Josh. 6:17; 7:10–11).

At the heart of this matter is the recognition that if Israel goes off into idolatry, she has effectively become paganized. Yahweh war, then, is essentially war against the imaginary gods of the world who challenge the sovereignty of Yahweh. In this sense, Yahweh war can perhaps more properly be termed deicide rather than homicide. Only by Yahweh's swift and complete defeat of false gods can his sovereignty be guarded and celebrated. It follows, then, that those who promote and practice the worship of other gods—Israelites included—must expect the fate of those gods, that is, total eradication. As the narrative here points out, the lesson to be learned from such harsh and uncompromising measures is that "Israel will hear and be afraid, and no one among you will do such an evil thing again" (Deut. 13:11).

---

[17]Kaminsky, "Joshua 7," 321, 338–45.

Joshua 6:1-27

The first application of Yahweh war occurs at Jericho at the very beginning of the Conquest.[18] Its cultic nature is seen in the presence of the priests with the ark of the covenant who lead the way on the seventh day (6:4) and sound the signal for the walls to collapse (6:20). Yahweh presents himself as the instigator of the campaign (6:2) and the one who makes it successful (6:16). The result is the utter destruction (*ḥrm*) of man and beast (6:21) and the burning (*śrp*) of the city itself (6:24). However, the things destroyed are here called *ḥerem*, that is, things (and people) devoted to Yahweh for his exclusive use.[19] Thus, the meanings "destroy" and "devote" both occur in the narrative.

Joshua 8:1-29

The next place to suffer Yahweh war is Ai, a strong military outpost northwest of Jericho. The narrative begins with the command not to fear, followed by Yahweh's assurance to be with Joshua and the people (8:1). This time, however, only the people of Ai are to be annihilated (*ḥrm*)—goods and livestock can be taken by Israel (8:2). Employing a strategy of ruses and ambushes, Joshua is able to set upon and capture all the men of Ai, whom he then slaughters to the last man (8:22), along with women and children (8:24-26). The structures of the city are then burned to the ground (8:28). The goods are spared, this time allocated to the Israelite people (8:27). The use of the verbs smiting (*nkh*, 8:22) and burning (*śrp*, 8:28), along with the use of *ḥrm*, is enough to show that Yahweh war is in view.

Joshua 10-11

Joshua's southern and northern campaigns consist of the application of Yahweh war. The alliance of Amorite kings against Israel comes about precisely because of the news about Ai's annihilation by *ḥrm* (10:1). One by one Joshua smites (*nkh*, 10:10, 26, 28, 30, 32, 33, 35, 37, 39, 40, 41) the southern kings and their

---

[18]Jeffrey H. Niehaus, "Joshua and Ancient Near Eastern Warfare," *JETS* 31 (1988): 37-50.

[19]Kaminsky, "Joshua 7," 329 n. 38.

cities. Yahweh is said to fight *(lḥm)* for Israel (10:14, 42), a clear indicator of the nature of these campaigns.

The northern campaign shares much in common with that of the south largely because of its nature as Yahweh war. There is the appeal not to fear (11:6; cf. 10:8), the promise that Yahweh will deliver (11:6) and its fulfillment (11:8), the smiting (11:8, 10, 11, 12, 14, 17), the burning (11:6, 9, 11, 13), and the total annihilation of human beings *(ḥrm,* 11:11, 12, 20, 21). In summarizing the conquest as a whole, the narrator makes the remarkable observation that all of Israel's victories come about because Yahweh has hardened the heart of their enemies, inducing them to attack his people so that he will thereby have occasion to annihilate them (11:20). Israel must show them no favor, for God intends these nations to be eliminated from the land.

1 Samuel 15:1–23

One of Saul's first assignments after assuming the kingship of Israel is to take vengeance against the Amalekites, who had made cowardly raids against the weak and infirm of Israel in the Sinai desert (Ex. 17:8–16). At that time, Yahweh commanded Moses to write a memorandum that he would someday completely blot out Amalek's memory (17:14). Four centuries later the time has come. The Lord's command to Saul (1 Sam. 15:2) is to go and smite *(nkh,* 15:3; cf. 15:7) Amalek and utterly decimate *(ḥrm,* 15:3) it. The *ḥerem* is to be total (15:3), but Saul spares the king of Amalek and the best of the animals and goods (15:9, 15, 21). This blatant disregard for the seriousness of Yahweh war costs Saul his throne, for to obey its requirements is far more important than to worship Yahweh with sacrifices (15:22–23).

Eschatological Texts

It is somewhat striking that though God's dealings with the nations in eschatological times are decidedly militaristic in flavor (Isa. 2:12–17; 9:1–7; 13:6–16; 24:1–13; 34:1–7; Jer. 25:32–38; Ezek. 25:1–7; Zech. 14:9–15; etc.), the technical terms and formulae associated with Yahweh war are few and far between. Isaiah 11:11–16, describing the return of Israel as a reenactment of the Exodus deliverance, speaks of the difficulties to be encountered as though they were the Red Sea, an enemy to be placed under *ḥrm* (11:15).[20] This, of course, is reminiscent of the role of Yahweh as warrior as celebrated in the Song of the Sea (Ex. 15:3–4, 6). It is he who, in the last days, will initiate the return of Israel and Judah to the land (Isa. 11:11), who will reconcile these two and restore them as one people (11:13), who will give them dominion over the nations (11:14), and who will pave the way of return to the Promised Land (11:16; cf. 19:23; 35:8; 40:3; 62:10).

Jeremiah also speaks of eschatological judgment in Yahweh-war terms. Addressing Babylon, he foresees a day when Babylon will suffer total destruction (*ḥrm*) in a battle led by Yahweh (Jer. 50:21–22). He will set a trap for this erstwhile scourge of the earth precisely because Babylon, as the symbol par excellence of anti-God rebellion, will dare to strive against his sovereignty (50:24). As warrior, Yahweh will deploy his weapons and marshal his heavenly hosts in order to accomplish his mission (50:25). The objective and result will be utter annihilation (*ḥrm*, 50:26). These texts point to a time more fully clarified and elaborated in the New Testament, where, as we will see, Yahweh-war sentiments continue to be important.

THE HISTORICAL, CULTURAL, AND THEOLOGICAL OCCASION FOR YAHWEH WAR

Having reviewed briefly the most important Yahweh-war texts with their technical terms and leading themes, it is important now to determine the circumstances that gave rise to such a phenomenon. Even a cursory survey of the data shows that Yahweh war as defined by the application of genocide originated in connection with the Exodus event and the subsequent occupation of the land promised to Israel's patriarchal ancestors.[21] But why were such extreme measures necessary, and what role did the devotion of places, persons, and things play in the overall concept of Yahweh war? The best way to approach the matter is to try to come to grips with the nature of the relationship between Yahweh and Israel, the nation on whose behalf

---

[20]Ollenburger, "Introduction," 27; Stern, *The Biblical Ḥerem*, 192.

[21]Millard Lind argues that the whole ground for Yahweh war is found in "Israel's testimony to a crucial event in early warfare itself—the exodus" (Lind, *Yahweh Is a Warrior*, 31).

such war was carried out, and to understand what issued from that relationship that could account for genocide as a remedy for guaranteeing stability in the relationship.

The Patriarchal Covenant and Promises

The remedy for the Fall and for human sinfulness included the calling out of a people through whom all the nations of the earth would be blessed.[22] This originated with Abraham, whom God sovereignly selected to found this nation (Gen. 12:1–3), with whom he entered into a covenant of grant (17:1–14), and to whom he gave the specific promise of a land (13:14–18; 15:7, 18–21; 17:8). Most important, Abraham's descendants would be God's people in a unique and special way, a relationship spelled out explicitly later on (17:7; Ex. 3:7, 10; 5:1; 6:7; etc.). It would be as their God that he would permit them to become slaves in a foreign land (Gen. 15:13), but it would also be as their God that he would rescue them and with great power bring them back to Canaan, the land of promise (15:14, 16).

Throughout the period of the patriarchs, the promises of blessing and land continued, but always with the ominous sense that the return to the land and its possession would be fraught with difficulty. If it were to happen, it would be because Yahweh would provide the leadership and resources (Gen. 22:16–17; 26:3; 28:1–4; 35:12; 46:2–4).

The Sonship of Israel and the Need for Deliverance

One of the most remarkable epithets to describe Israel in the Old Testament is that of Yahweh's son (Ex. 4:22–23; cf. Isa. 63:16; 64:8; Hos. 11:1). Already identified as God's people, they found refuge, then bondage, in Egypt—a situation that went from oppression (Ex. 1:11, 13–14) to infanticide (1:15–16). Into this intolerable turn of events steps Israel's God. He hears the groans of his people, remembers the covenant he made with their fathers, and undertakes measures to effect their redemption (2:23–24; 3:7–8). He will now assume the role of warrior, first of all demonstrating his glory and power to Pharaoh (3:10),

---

[22]H. Eberhard von Waldow, "The Concept of War in the Old Testament," *HBT* 6 (1984): 46.

and when that fails by itself to achieve the desired ends, he will implement by force the deliverance of his beleaguered people (3:17, 20; 6:1, 6–8; 7:4; 12:17, 37–42).[23]

The warlike nature of Yahweh's redemption of Israel finds special meaning in the intimacy of his covenant relationship with them as Father to son. Moses is commissioned to inform Pharaoh, the personification of the whole nation of Egypt, that Israel is Yahweh's firstborn son, his heir, as it were, and that as such Israel must be free to fulfill its task of serving as Yahweh's means of blessing all the earth (Ex. 4:22). The penalty for refusing to let Israel go will be the death of Pharaoh's own firstborn son (4:23). Despite the devastating plagues against Egypt that nearly ruin the country, Pharaoh refuses to comply. Thus, Yahweh's edict goes forth—all of Egypt's firstborn sons must die (11:5), a judgment that falls on every family that fails to avail itself of the protective blood of the Passover lamb (12:29–30). From that time on every firstborn male of Israel must be devoted to Yahweh as a token of his redeeming grace in preserving his firstborn son Israel (13:2, 11–16; 22:29; 34:20; Num. 3:12–13, 40–51; 8:14–19).

Also not to be overlooked is the fundamental fact that the conflict in Egypt is not really between Yahweh and Pharaoh or even Yahweh and Egypt, but between Yahweh and the gods of Egypt (Ex. 12:12; Num. 33:4).[24] Yahweh war is at its base a war against spiritual darkness and wickedness in realms that transcend the human and earthly (Gen. 3:15; Job 1:6–12; 2:2–6). The Song of the Sea ought to be understood in these terms, for it not only celebrates Yahweh's triumph over Pharaoh and his armies (Ex. 15:1, 4–5) but also has clear overtones of an even more profound and significant victory, one over every competing notion of deity real or imaginary. "Who among the gods is like you, O

---

[23]Craigie, *The Problem of War in the Old Testament*, 11, 94–97; idem, "Yahweh Is a Man of War," *SJT* 22 (1969): 184; F. M. Cross, "The Divine Warrior in Israel's Early Cult," in *Biblical Motifs, Origins and Transformations*, ed. A. Altmann (Cambridge, Mass.: Harvard Univ. Press, 1966), 19–21; Lind, *Yahweh Is a Warrior*, 88; T. Longman III, "The Divine Warrior: The New Testament Use of an Old Testament Motif," *WTJ* 44 (1982): 292–306; Weinfeld, "Divine Intervention in War in Ancient Israel and in the Ancient Near East," 121.

[24]Jeffrey J. Niehaus, "The Warrior and His God: The Covenant Foundation of History and Historiography," in *Faith, Tradition, and History*, ed. A. R. Millard, James K. Hoffmeier, and David W. Baker (Winona Lake, Ind.: Eisenbrauns, 1994), 308.

LORD," asks the poet. "Who is like you—majestic in holiness, awesome in glory, working wonders?" (15:11). Yahweh has prevailed over Egypt, it is true, but he also has proven his sovereignty over all aspirants to sovereignty, whether human or divine.

The Conquest: War in Fulfillment of Promise

Yahweh war was necessary to Israel's escape from Egypt, and it will be necessary to her conquest and settlement of Canaan. Whereas the former is more inferential, the latter is spelled out in unmistakable terms. The issue is the same, however, in both cases: God has promised the patriarchs that their national descendants will be delivered from onerous bondage to a hostile power and brought to a land that they will own and occupy. All this will be initiated and carried to successful conclusion by their warrior God, the Lord of Hosts, who will wage battle against overwhelming odds on their behalf.

The prescription for Yahweh war. Like anything else in the purpose and plan of God, there must be a protocol to be followed in carrying out Yahweh war. No one passage in the Old Testament presents a comprehensive and systematic outline of how this was to be undertaken, though we have examined a number of texts that, taken together, provide a reasonably good understanding. In addition to these, we must here examine Deuteronomy 7:1–5.

The setting of this passage is the plains of Moab on the eve of the conquest of Canaan under Joshua. Israel has already enjoyed success in conquering Transjordanian kingdoms and is beginning to occupy their territories (Deut. 3:12–17). Now Moses turns his attention to the west. He reminds the people that Yahweh has already given them the land—at least in promise—and that he will do to the kings in Canaan what he did to Sihon of Heshbon and Og of Bashan. Yahweh "your God himself will fight for you" (3:22; cf. 1:30). That is, Yahweh is the warrior who, according to his own strategy and by his own power, will bring success.

The enemy consists of seven nations, seven no doubt reflecting the fullness of opposition.[25] Their description as being

---

[25] A. D. H. Mayes, *Deuteronomy* (NCBC; Grand Rapids: Eerdmans, 1979), 182.

more populous and powerful than Israel heightens the idea of their invincibility (7:1). If Israel is to prevail, it will be only by divine assistance. This notion of vast enemy superiority is, in fact, one of the hallmarks of Yahweh war.

The order of events is of significance. It is after Yahweh delivers over (*ntn*) the enemy to them that Israel will be able to smite (*nkh*) them. And the smiting must result in *ḥerem*, utter destruction (7:2). The option of making covenant with such people or undertaking marriage with them or even of showing mercy and sparing them for some other reason can never be entertained. They will induce Israel to follow their gods and embrace their abominable forms of worship (7:4). Instead, they and their worship apparatus must be exterminated (7:5).

The introduction of Yahweh-war legislation so early in Deuteronomy can be explained by its near juxtaposition to the commandments to have no other gods and to desist from making and worshiping pagan idols (Deut. 5:7–10).[26] These commandments are adumbrated by the Shema formula ("The LORD our God, the LORD is one") and the command that he is to be worshiped exclusively and fully (6:4–5). Hard against these claims is the injunction to destroy utterly those who subvert Yahweh's sovereign lordship. Yahweh war is war in defense of his unique demands on his people. To worship other gods is an act of high treason, one deserving of death (13:15). By extension, those who induce God's people to such disloyalty are also worthy of death.

The passage following these prescriptions in Deuteronomy 7 is also important to the case being made here. Here Israel is called a "holy" people, that is, one set apart for God's special purpose (7:6). They have been divinely elected and delivered from bondage in fulfillment of the promises to the fathers. Their success depends on their obedience to the covenant (7:12), especially the exclusive worship of their God (7:16) and the destruction of the nations intent on leading them astray (7:24–25). So important is this to Yahweh that he himself will lead in their defeat and utter destruction (7:19–23).

The implementation of Yahweh war. The first application of Yahweh war following its Deuteronomic prescription is the

---

[26]Jeffrey H. Tigay, *Deuteronomy* (JPSTC; Philadelphia: The Jewish Publication Society, 1996), 84.

conquest of Jericho. After careful planning of strategy in which spies are sent to reconnoiter the area (Josh. 2:1–24), Joshua proceeds to take Jericho in line with divine direction. The preparation already shows signs of the character of the impending conflict. The Canaanite Rahab discloses that she is aware that Yahweh has determined to give Israel the land (2:9) and that he will do so in terms reminiscent of the Exodus deliverance and the annihilation of the Transjordanian cities (2:10). She, at least, has learned from this that Yahweh is God (cf. Deut. 4:32–35).

Preparation for the conquest of Jericho involves the role of the priests with the ark of the covenant (Josh. 3:1–17). The ark represents God's tangible presence (Ex. 25:22; 30:6) and therefore symbolizes his leadership in the struggle that lies ahead. When the priestly procession moves forward into the Jordan, the waters cease flowing and the riverbed becomes dry, just as the Red Sea did when Yahweh led his people out of Egypt (Josh. 3:14–17; cf. Ex. 14:15–22). Once across the river, the priests bearing the ark circumvent the city of Jericho once a day for six days and then seven times on the seventh day (Josh. 6:4). The importance of the ark in identifying the presence of God and thus of Yahweh war is clear from the fact that it is mentioned ten times in the narrative (6:1–16).

At a signal, the trumpets sound, and the city walls collapse, enabling the hosts of Israel to enter and to annihilate (ḥrm) the population and all animal life (Josh. 6:20–21). Only the precious metals are spared, everything else being consigned to the flames (6:24). These goods become ḥerem, but not in the sense of being destroyed. Rather, they are devoted to Yahweh by being placed in the sacred treasury. The juxtaposition of ḥrm in the sense of dedication to Yahweh (6:17–18) and in the sense of destruction (6:21) is instructive. Both are elements of Yahweh war, but in the one case the result is annihilation and in the other preservation. However, the preservation is for the benefit not of human beings but of Yahweh, for the practical maintenance of the cultus.

Disregard of this aspect of Yahweh war brings most serious consequences, as is seen in the appropriation by Achan of the goods of Jericho that were to have been devoted to Yahweh alone (7:1). It is viewed as a violation of God's covenant (7:11; cf. Lev. 27:28); in fact, it is theft, and until it is dealt with, Israel can no longer expect successful prosecution of Yahweh war (Josh. 7:12).

The remedy is harsh, indeed. The person guilty of the deed must suffer *ḥerem*; that is, he must be devoted to Yahweh by death (7:15), a fate that befalls not only Achan but his entire family (7:25–26).

The purpose of Yahweh war in the case of Jericho is not so much to eliminate the gods and cultus of its inhabitants as to elevate Yahweh in the view of his own people. He wants them to know that he is their God as he, the God of all the earth (Josh. 2:11), is present with them to accomplish the work of conquest (2:10). It follows, moreover, that all the peoples of the earth will recognize that Israel's God is God indeed (4:24).

THE JUSTIFICATION OF OLD TESTAMENT YAHWEH WAR

It is one thing to provide a sketch of the nature and history of Yahweh war in the Old Testament. It is quite another to understand it in terms of the character of God and to justify it in light of the teachings of Jesus and the New Testament, to say nothing of modern notions of ethics and morality.[27] In a day when genocide and ethnic cleansing rightly stand condemned by all morally sensitive people, how can anyone—and the Christian in particular—defend its practice at any time, even in the ancient Old Testament past? The answer to these troubling questions must lie in a proper appreciation of the true nature of God, the opposition to his eternal purposes, and the means by which this opposition can and must be overcome.

God the Protagonist

A study this brief cannot possibly do justice to the subject of theology proper, so attention must be focused on those facets of God's nature, character, and purposes most pertinent to the issue at hand, namely, his role as protagonist in the prosecution of Yahweh war. If anything is clear in the foregoing review of this phenomenon, it is that such war was conceived by God,

---

[27]These kinds of concerns are addressed by, among others, Craigie, *The Problem of War in the Old Testament*, 100–102; idem, "Yahweh Is a Man of War," 186–88; Firestone, "Conceptions of Holy War in Biblical and Qur'anic Tradition," 100; Jeph Holloway, "The Ethical Dilemma of the Holy War," *SWJT* 41 (1998): 63.

commanded by him, executed by him, and brought by him alone to successful conclusion. Among the attributes associated with his participation in Yahweh war are God's omnipotence, his infinite wisdom, and, above all, his holiness. In fact, it is this last-mentioned characteristic that gave rise to earlier descriptions of this kind of conflict as "holy war."

All this is not to negate such divine virtues as love, grace, mercy, and forbearance; indeed, these and other elements of the wholeness of God as articulated in classic Christian theology are also found in his work of Yahweh war, albeit in more hidden and implicit ways. But holiness looms largest as the prism through which to view the harsh reality of genocide at the hands of a wrathful and powerful God. Biblical texts are replete with references to God's holiness (Lev. 11:44–45; 19:2; 20:7, 26; 21:8; Josh. 24:19; 1 Sam. 2:2; 6:20; Ps. 22:3; 99:3, 5, 9; Isa. 5:16; 6:3; 57:15).

At the same time, none of the passages prescribing or narrating Yahweh war explicitly refers to God's holiness. Instead, the focus is on the holiness of Israel, the people set apart to reflect the character of Yahweh and to carry out his salvific design (Ex. 19:6; Deut. 7:6; 14:2, 21; 26:19; 28:9). A comprehensive theological overview yields the conclusion that Israel must be holy because Yahweh is holy and that one of the major purposes of Yahweh war was to protect that holiness.

The Enemy

God's holiness does not exist in a vacuum, as only an abstract quality. He is holy because he stands apart from that which is not; in fact, his holiness opposes everything and everyone that falls short of his perfection. All that God created was declared to be "good," that is, without flaw or any hint of hostility toward the Creator (Gen. 1:31). But the Fall and the mystery of sin put an end to that, and at both the heavenly and earthly levels a rupture occurred between God and creation, a division perpetuated by rebellious antagonism toward God and his purposes. The warning to the serpent that there would be enmity between it and the human race, culminating ultimately in the serpent's defeat (Gen. 3:15), suggests a conflict of a higher order, a contest of wills between God and the spiritual forces that strive against him for dominion.

Another word for this conflict is war, a *Leitmotif* coursing through the narrative of sacred history from beginning to end. Yahweh war is, in one sense then, a struggle against the realms of evil on a massive, transcendent level, an engagement that commences with the first creaturely hubris and that will end only when Satan and his minions are fully eradicated from God's kingdom.[28] At another and more limited level, it is war connected historically to the struggle for Israel's emancipation from Egypt and their conquest and settlement of the land of Canaan. Careful reading of this more limited account will, however, reveal its inextricable linkage to the larger, more cosmic conflict.[29] Pharaoh and Egypt become ciphers for Satan and his kingdom, and the Canaanite nations symbolize the kingdoms of evil yet to be defeated and dispossessed. Such foes cannot be pacified, nor can one reach accommodation with them. They are hopelessly in rebellion and must be held to account firmly and with finality.

This interpretation of sacred history accounts for a number of things relative to Yahweh war. (1) It explains why the eradication of idolatry is almost a sine qua non of its successful prosecution. Idolatry is in its essence the proclamation of the existence of supernatural powers that coexist with the God of creation and that demand that worship should be tendered also to them. As we have noted repeatedly, idolatry is defiance of the first two commandments that assert that only Yahweh is to be Israel's God and that no images are to be made of any creature with the intent of bowing down to worship them.

(2) Once it is recognized that the battle ultimately is cosmic and that what is at stake is God's reputation and sovereignty, it is easier to see why radical destruction of those who oppose him is an absolute necessity. The matter cannot be left only on the spiritual plane. Human agents in the employ of supernatural handlers must also suffer the same fate if they remain unrepentant.

(3) This leads to further consideration of the peoples particularly singled out in the Old Testament as those condemned to the judgment of Yahweh war. Though all nations are in rebellion against God, in the outworking of God's purposes in history

---

[28]Craigie, *The Problem of War in the Old Testament*, 40–42.

[29]Daniel G. Reid and Tremper Longman III, *God Is a Warrior* (Grand Rapids: Zondervan, 1995), 72–78.

those that most directly confront his chosen people Israel are especially subject to his judgment. In God's providence he led Israel to Egypt and then delivered them in a powerful display of military might. Yahweh war in this phase was limited in that Egypt, though punished, was allowed to survive, for idolatry was not fundamentally at issue. The Canaanite nations, by contrast, were in illegal occupation of the land God had promised to Abraham and his descendants. Moreover, they were irretrievably lost to anti-God idolatry and were certain to proselytize Israel to do the same. Yahweh war for them had to result in their utter annihilation lest these fatal consequences for Israel come to pass.

That Yahweh war was to be employed against the Canaanites was not an ad hoc decision that arose on the eve of the Conquest. One must reach far back into the history of God's involvement with these people in order more fully to appreciate why they were singled out. Apart from their appearance in the genealogies, the Canaanites are first mentioned in Noah's curse of Canaan, Ham's youngest son (Gen. 9:25–27).[30] There it is said that Canaan would be the lowliest of servants to his brothers, especially of Shem. The ominous significance of this threat runs as a thread through Israel's early history. When Abraham reached the land of Canaan, he found that "the Canaanites were in the land" (Gen. 12:6; cf. 13:7). This, of course, was from the standpoint of Moses, who was reflecting on the fact that the Canaanites were in the land in his own day but not in the hill country as in patriarchal times (Num. 13:29). Even more ominous is the notation spoken to Abraham that Israel's return to the land of Canaan following the Egyptian sojourn would be delayed for more than four hundred years or until the iniquity of the Amorites was complete (Gen. 15:16). Its being complete suggests that it was beyond remedy and could therefore be dealt with only by destruction.[31]

Long before Moses prohibited marriage with the Canaanites, Abraham had forbidden his son Isaac from doing so (Gen. 24:3). His great-grandson Judah was not above breaking this taboo, however, and took for himself a Canaanite bride, much to his grief (38:2, 26). Much later, Israel encountered Canaanites

[30]Allen P. Ross, *Creation and Blessing* (Grand Rapids: Baker, 1988), 218–20.

[31]Victor P. Hamilton, *The Book of Genesis: Chapters 1–17* (NICOT; Grand Rapids: Eerdmans, 1990), 436.

(Num. 21:1–3) and Amorites (21:10–35) en route to the land of promise. They were able to defeat them and even to occupy Amorite territory in the Transjordan. In pursuit of the lands to the west, Joshua declared that the expulsion of the Canaanites there would testify that the living God was among his people (Josh. 3:10). Then, in fulfillment of the Noahic curse, the Canaanites of Ephraim became menial slaves of Israel, the offspring of Shem (Josh. 16:10; cf. 9:22–27; 17:13). Ever after, it became proverbial to speak of Israel's stubborn rebellion against God as akin to the wickedness of the Amorites, the standard by which to measure godlessness (2 Kings 21:11; Ezra 9:1).

Israel: The Divine Instrument

Israel's role in the implementation of Yahweh war needs careful attention because *only Israel was authorized to carry it out in Old Testament times.* The reason for this dubious privilege is clear: Israel was the elect people of God, chosen not just to mediate the message of salvation to the world but also to serve as his agent in bringing to pass his will on the earth. At times, notably in the years of the Conquest, this divinely ordained task would require the taking up of arms as the army of God. It is not as though he could not achieve his objectives on his own, for, in fact, more often than not the undertaking and success in Yahweh war is attributed to God himself and not to Israel or any other human agency. But the fact remains that Israel was involved—and only Israel out of all the nations of the earth.

Thus, it follows that Israel would be a special target of opposition by those who were alienated from Israel's God. But since Yahweh wars were mainly, if not exclusively, wars of aggression, Israel would be perceived as aggressors, with all the onus that entails.[32] Quite likely, then, when Israel undertook war against an enemy, there was no inkling that Yahweh was really the protagonist and Israel only a bit player. Only when it was apparent that the outcome could be explained in no other way would Israel's foes realize that they had done battle against Israel's God himself (Ex. 15:14–15; Deut. 2:15; Josh. 2:9, 11, 24; Hab. 3:7). The reaction, then, would be either to fear and submit or to become more stiff and resistant to God's judgment.

---

[32]Jones, "The Concept of Holy War," 303, 305; Ollenburger, "Introduction," 21.

The fact that Israel alone was the elect nation charged with such astounding privilege and responsibility means that Israel alone could prosecute Yahweh war as a righteous act. And even Israel could do so only when God gave special mandate and instruction in each case. The mere performance of ritual or use of artifacts, such as the ark of the covenant, could not guarantee success or even qualify the engagement as Yahweh war (see, e.g., Num. 14:39–45; 1 Sam. 4:1–11). If God was not in it, no amount of human strength and strategy could achieve God's objectives. The ramifications of this for the issue of war in general and war conducted under the guise of divine direction in particular are immense. If no case could be made for Yahweh war without Israel's participation in Old Testament times, surely none can be made today whether done in the name of Christ, Allah, or any other authority.

Yahweh War: The Divine Means

As the omnipotent One, God can accomplish his purposes in any way that pleases him. Usually he uses human instruments, however, a principle much in line with the creation mandate of Genesis 1:26–28. This is the case with the prosecution of Yahweh war, for though God himself initiated, led, and brought success to the effort, Israel was very much a partner. The result brought glory to God but also a recognition among the nations that Israel was a highly favored people (Deut. 4:32–40; 11:24–26; Josh. 2:8–14; 9:9–10, 24). In a more practical sense, the extreme measure of Yahweh war was necessary for at least four reasons: (1) the irremediable hardness of the hearts of its victims; (2) the need to protect Israel against spiritual corruption; (3) the destruction of idolatry; and (4) the education of Israel and the nations as to the character and intentions of the one true God.

Hardness of heart. A number of terms are used in the Old Testament to speak of the condition of stubborn resistance to God's will, a state described figuratively as a hardening of the heart.[33] The general result is the inability of individuals in this condition to respond favorably to the overtures of God's grace, leaving them open to nothing but God's awesome judgment.

---

[33]See Robert B. Chisholm Jr., "Divine Hardening in the Old Testament," Bib-Sac 153 (1996): 410–34.

The process begins with one's hardening of oneself and ends with the confirmation of that hardening by the Lord, who then brings about the only avenue available to him—the destruction of the irredeemable rebel. Only God knows when that kind of hardening has occurred; therefore, only God could decree the imposition of Yahweh war or other retributive measures.

A classic case of such hardening is that of Pharaoh, who, when commanded to release Israel from bondage, refused to do so. God told Moses ahead of time that he would harden Pharaoh's heart (Ex. 4:21; 7:3), a threat that came to pass time after a time (9:12; 10:1, 20, 27; 11:10; 14:8). However, Pharaoh himself invited this hardening by his own willful rejection of God's pleas and warnings to let Israel go (7:13, 14, 22; 8:15, 19, 32; 9:7, 34). The alternation between Pharaoh's self-hardening and that brought on him by the Lord is not easy to disentangle, but the overall process is clear: Pharaoh, by his own free will, withstood the demands of Israel's God and thereby invoked on himself a spirit of unrepentance that could lead only to judgment.

The Conquest narratives also make plain that a rationale for Yahweh war was a hardening of heart and spirit on the part of God's enemies. King Sihon of Heshbon, for example, refused to let Israel pass through his land, for Yahweh had hardened his heart and made him stubborn in spirit so that he could fall into Israel's hands (Deut. 2:30). That this was not an isolated case is clear from the summary statement of Joshua 11:20, where it is said of the Conquest as a whole that "it was the LORD himself who hardened their hearts to wage war against Israel, so that he might destroy them totally [ḥrm], exterminating them without mercy, as the LORD had commanded Moses." The moral and theological implications of this are profound, but it is most apparent that those subject to Yahweh war were deserving of it, for their condition of rebellion—no matter how it came about—left no alternative.[34]

Protection of Israel. An important justification for Yahweh war was the need for God's chosen people to be preserved from the inroads of paganism that would surely insinuate themselves, were Israel to coexist with the Canaanite nations in the land of promise. The prescriptive text (Deut. 7:1–5) underscores the fact

---

[34]Richard S. Hess, *Joshua: An Introduction and Commentary* (TOTC; Leicester, England: Inter-Varsity Press, 1996), 218.

that alliance of any kind with the inhabitants of Canaan would result in Israel's falling away from Yahweh into idolatry and thus under his judgment (7:4; cf. 7:25–26; 8:11–20; 28:15–19; 30:15–20). The same point is made in Deuteronomy 20:16–18, where Yahweh enjoins the eradication of the Canaanites lest they teach Israel to emulate their abominable religious practices. This would be "sin against the LORD your God" (20:18). Just as Israel had descended into Egypt to be isolated from Canaanite corruption (Gen. 45:5–8; 50:20), so the Canaanites were to be dispossessed in order for Israel to carry out its responsibility as God's covenant nation.

Eradication of idolatry. In line with the preceding purpose for Yahweh war is the removal not only of pagan nations that practiced idolatry but the extermination of idolatry itself. While theoretically heathenism can exist in the abstract, that is, apart from its proponents, in Israel's experience idolatry was linked to peoples and nations with whom she came in contact. This is why its removal was contingent on the destruction of those nations. The Decalogue, in both its renditions, places the prohibition of idolatry immediately after the declaration that only Yahweh is God (Ex. 20:4–6; Deut. 5:8–10). This juxtaposition emphatically underscores the stark distinction between the one and only true God and human representations of false gods.[35] For Israel to acknowledge and worship these imaginary deities would be corrupting (Deut. 4:15–16) and would result in Israel's demise (4:23–28). Therefore, idolatry must be uprooted along with the nations that embrace it and induce Israel to do likewise (7:5, 16, 25; 12:2–3).

Education of Israel and the nations. The pedagogical value of Yahweh war is that its display of God's power and wrath on the one hand, and of his grace and glory on the other, would lead both Israel and the nations of the earth to recognize his sovereignty, especially in connection with and on behalf of his chosen people. God had told Moses that the Exodus would convince Israel that Yahweh is God (Ex. 6:6–7; cf. 7:17; 16:12). Likewise, Pharaoh and the Egyptians would acknowledge this truth in the plagues and in Israel's subsequent departure (7:5; 14:4, 18). The conquest of Canaan would achieve the same results.

---

[35]Umberto Cassuto, *A Commentary on the Book of Exodus*, trans. Israel Abrahams (Jerusalem: Magnes, 1967), 242.

Rahab knew that Israel's God was God of all peoples even before her city, Jericho, fell, for she had heard of his exploits in Egypt and the Transjordan (Josh. 2:9–11). Joshua declared that the Jordan had dried up so that Israel might fear God and the nations might confess his power and preeminence (Josh. 4:23–24).

YAHWEH WAR AND THE NEW TESTAMENT

Space constraints prohibit any discussion of the concept of Yahweh war in postbiblical Jewish literature, though clearly it was a matter of interest. A major Dead Sea scroll text is dedicated to such a theme, the so-called *War Scroll* (1QM), and the apocryphal and pseudepigraphical writings also address the matter in various places (Jdt. 5:13; Wisd. 10:18; 19:7; Sir. 10:13; 48:21; 1 Macc. 4:9–11; 2 Macc. 5:1–4; 10:24–31; 11:6; 12:15–16; *1 Enoch* 1:9; 56:5–8). The major contribution of such writings is the advancement they make on Old Testament apocalyptic themes and imagery relative to end-time events, most especially the climactic battles that result in God's ultimate victory over the forces of darkness and evil (see Dan. 2:36–45; 7:23–28; 12:1–4; Zech. 14:1–21).[36]

The New Testament draws from this conceptual and literary environment as well, particularly in its apocalyptic teachings.[37] Discussion here will be limited to Jesus' Olivet Discourse (Matt. 24:3–31; Mark 13:3–27; Luke 21:5–28) and the Apocalypse (Rev. 6:1–8; 12:7–17; 16:12–16; 19:11–21; 20:7–10). In line with the theme of this chapter, the focus will be on Yahweh-war elements, if any, that find roots in the Old Testament. If such exist, to what extent can it be said that Yahweh war has ongoing relevance to eschatological times and, perhaps, even to the present age of the church?[38]

When the disciples asked Jesus about the destruction of Herod's temple, the sign of his second coming, and the consummation of the present age (Matt. 24:3), he launched into a discourse concerning events that must occur before the "end"

---

[36]Reid and Longman, *God Is a Warrior*, 63–71.

[37]T. R. Hobbs, *A Time for War: A Study of Warfare in the Old Testament* (Wilmington, Del.: Michael Glazier, 1989), 208–33.

[38]See especially Reid and Longman, *God Is a Warrior*, 92–118; I. Howard Marshall, "New Testament Perspectives on War," *EvQ* 57 (1985): 115, 117.

could come.[39] The fall of the temple in A.D. 70 would be only typical of the traumatic and utter ruin the world could expect at the end of the age. Among the indicators of the end or its nearness are famines and earthquakes (Matt. 24:7; Mark 13:8; Luke 21:11), the rise of false prophets (Matt. 24:11; Mark 13:22), signs and wonders such as the darkening of the sun (Matt. 24:24, 29; Mark 13:24; Luke 21:25), the appearance of angels blowing trumpets (Matt. 24:31; Mark 13:27), a great tribulation that is unprecedented in world history (Matt. 24:21; Mark 13:19; Luke 21:23), the abomination that brings desolation (Matt. 24:15; Mark 13:14), and the sign of the "Son of Man" (Matt. 24:30; Mark 13:26; Luke 21:27).

It is significant that Jesus makes no reference in this lengthy discourse to anything resembling Old Testament Yahweh war, though clearly he describes an age of incredible persecution and distress. Even Luke's account, which speaks of military conflict, hardly paints it in Yahweh-war terms. One can only conclude from Jesus' teaching that such war, though common in the Old Testament, has no place in the age of the church—at least, no legitimate place.[40] The same is true of the New Testament letters. There is abundant military imagery, but nearly always the conflict is in the realm of the spiritual (1 Cor. 9:26; 2 Cor. 7:5; 10:3; 1 Tim. 1:18; 6:12; 2 Tim. 2:4; 4:7).[41]

The Apocalypse, however, describes a number of scenes in which Yahweh war reminiscent of that of the Old Testament will be waged.[42] During the Great Tribulation, riders will go forth on horses symbolic of conquest, slaughter, famine, and death, and they will wreak havoc on the earth (Rev. 6:1–8). These are clearly agents of the Almighty, for it is the Lamb who opens the seals of judgment, allowing this awesome destruction to take place (6:1). The imagery is drawn from the apocalyptic visions of the Old Testament prophet Zechariah, who foresaw Yahweh's dominion over the earth in highly militaristic terms (Zech. 1:7–11; 6:1–8).

The battle scene of Revelation 12:7–17 is even more precise in identifying the combatants. An "enormous red dragon" (12:3),

[39]Reid and Longman, God Is a Warrior, 126–27.

[40]Longman "The Divine Warrior," 292–302.

[41]Ibid., 302; Marshall, "New Testament Perspectives on War," 118.

[42]Adela Y. Collins, "The Political Perspective of the Revelation to John," JBL 96 (1977): 246–48; Hobbs, A Time for War, 233; Reid and Longman, God Is a Warrior, 180.

identified later as "the devil, or Satan" (12:9), is intent on destroying the child of a woman about to give birth, but before he can do so, the child is caught up into heaven (12:5). Meanwhile, the woman is sustained in the desert for three and a half years (12:6), following which the archangel Michael and the armies of heaven go to war with Satan. Satan is defeated and cast down to the earth, but he is not yet destroyed, for he begins, unsuccessfully, to persecute the woman and her offspring. This account makes clear that war between the righteous and the wicked on earth—whether on the physical (Old Testament) or spiritual (New Testament) level—is a historical, mundane working out of the cosmic struggle between God and Satan on the cosmic level.

The famous battle of Armageddon, to be fought at the end of the Great Tribulation period, is introduced in Revelation 16:12–16 and elaborated on in 19:11–21. In the former passage, the dragon spews out demonic spirits that gather the armies of the earth to do battle in "the battle on the great day of God Almighty" (16:14). The place of the battle is Armageddon (16:16), clearly the site of the conflict described also in 17:13–14 and 19:11–21. In the latter account, the heavenly warrior, known here also as "the Word of God" and the "King of kings and Lord of lords" (19:13, 16), descends on a white horse accompanied by the armies of heaven. He comes to reign over the earth (19:15), but to do so he must crush the assembled armies of humankind led by the beast and the false prophet (19:20; cf. 11:7; 13:1; 16:13). He does so and then inaugurates his millennial reign (20:4–6). That this is an apocalyptic version of Yahweh war is clear from the fact that it is initiated by Yahweh, carried out by him, and results in his victory and enthronement.

Finally, the culmination of the ages-long conflict between Yahweh and the forces of evil takes place after the Millennium in another display of Yahweh war (Rev. 20:7–10). Satan, having been freed from his thousand-year confinement, will make one more attempt to usurp God's sovereignty and overcome God's people, but to no avail. He and his hosts will be destroyed in this last battle, and all God's enemies will be consigned to everlasting judgment (20:11–14). Then will come the new heavens and earth, in which the perfect creation purposes of God will prevail forever.

THE CHRISTIAN AND YAHWEH WAR

The case presented here has been that of moderate discontinuity—that is, the view that Yahweh war as articulated in the Old Testament has no justification in the age of the church except in terms of spiritual conflict. The eschatological texts of the New Testament, however, as well as those of the Old, provide clear evidence for a resumption of Yahweh war in the end times, war to be understood in physical as well as spiritual terms. Yahweh war, then, is descriptive of the ages-old struggle between the sovereign God of Israel and the church on the one hand, and the devil and his demonic and human hosts on the other. Sometimes it is expressed in overt, physical, historical ways and sometimes (in the present age) in figurative and symbolic ways. It is the abuse of or confusion between these dispensational distinctions that has raised many issues in regard to the whole question of the Christian and war. Only some of these issues can receive treatment here, and only briefly.

War and the New Testament

An overwhelming impression from a careful reading of the Gospels is the advocacy of pacifism. Jesus did not counsel violence, promote it in any way, or condone it when his followers were inclined otherwise. Nevertheless, he never condemned war in any systematic way; in fact, he recognized its inevitability in both human experience and as a means of achieving God's eschatological purposes (Matt. 22:7; Luke 11:21–22; 14:31–32; 19:27). The same can be said of the apostles, though with a little more ambivalence (1 Cor. 9:7; 14:8; 2 Tim. 2:4; Heb. 7:1). Paul especially recognized the importance of human government in establishing and maintaining public tranquility, and he acknowledged that war sometimes is necessary to the accomplishment of this end (Rom. 13:1–7). He even went so far as to urge submission to government, a submission that surely involved the duty to bear arms and otherwise contribute to the well-being of society (Titus 3:1). Neither Jesus nor the apostles, however, sanctioned or otherwise endorsed what we have called Yahweh war. They clearly understood that in the "age of the Gentiles," such a resort was inappropriate and uncalled for.[43]

---

[43]Marshall, "New Testament Perspectives on War," 99–113.

The Christian and Pacifism

The stance toward war in the history of Christendom has run the gamut from an absolute refusal to bear arms under any circumstances to such militaristic enterprises as the Crusades with their overt claims to divine sanction in the spirit of biblical holy war.[44] Most Christians resist both extremes and find themselves comfortable with the notion of "just war," or at least war in defense of one's own country.[45] It is the contention of this paper that the Christian must, in this instance, be guided not by the Old Testament principles and practices of Yahweh war, for they were relevant to the Israelite theocracy only and pertinent primarily to the dispossession and/or annihilation of the Canaanite peoples, who illegally occupied the land of promise. Nor can the believer appeal to eschatological texts, which again, in our view, relate to a regathered Israel—at least initially—and then to the millennial age.

Having said this, we prefer to come down on the side of those who understand the Christian to be a citizen of two realms—the earthly and the heavenly—with their respective privileges and responsibilities. In a fallen world this sometimes means that the believer must take sword in hand in defense of home and country in recognition of the fact that the "[human] authorities that exist have been established by God" (Rom. 13:1). The presumption in all cases must be, of course, that the cause is right and just, for there is for the Christian a higher authority and moral claim: "We must obey God rather than men" (Acts 5:29).

The Christian and Genocide

The term *genocide* (lit., "killing of a people") has become part of the popular lexicon of the past half-century, primarily because of its application to the systematic slaughter of the Jewish people by German Nazism. Other, less well-known examples include the massacre of millions of Armenians by the Turks, the slaughter by

---

[44]Susan Niditch, *War in the Hebrew Bible: A Study in the Ethics of Violence* (New York: Oxford Univ. Press, 1993), 4–5; Craigie, *The Problem of War in the Old Testament*, 27–28.

[45]Craigie, *The Problem of War in the Old Testament*, 52–53; Niditch, *War in the Hebrew Bible*, 25–27; Derek Kidner, "Old Testament Perspectives on War," *EvQ* 57 (1985): 108.

the Russians and Chinese of multitudes of their own people, and the "ethnic cleansing" that has been carried out in the Balkans, central Africa, and other regions of the world. What is seldom acknowledged (or even understood) is that Yahweh war and its use of *herem* was also genocide, by both design and practice.

The issue, then, cannot be whether or not genocide is intrinsically good or evil—its sanction by a holy God settles that question. Rather, the issue has to do with the purpose of genocide, its initiator, and the particular circumstances of its application. We argued here that biblical genocide was part of a Yahweh-war policy enacted for a unique situation, directed against a certain people, and in line with the character of God himself, a policy whose design is beyond human comprehension but one that is not, for that reason, unjust or immoral. Those very limitations preclude any possible justification for modern genocide for any reason.

THE CHRISTIAN AND JIHAD

The term *holy war* has found fresh currency with the rise of militant Islam and its claims in some quarters that terrorist activities in its name fall under the rubric *jihad*. Though some argue that the Arabic word means nothing more than inner spiritual struggle or the like, scholarly consensus holds that it has also to do with aggressive, militant action in defense of and for the propagation of the Muslim faith.[46] The evidence of the Qur'an itself is conflicting. Some passages advocate a pacifist position in the face of controversy (Sura 15:94–95); others permit defensive war, especially against the citizens of Medina who threatened Muhammad and his Meccan followers (Sura 22:39–40); still others sanction wars of preemption or aggression (Sura 2:191, 217). Eventually—and in line with the Muslim conquest of the Middle East, North Africa, and Europe—full-scale *jihad* was enjoined as a means of propagating the faith (Sura 2:16; 9:5, 29). These various points of view reflect different periods in the history and development of the Islamic movement.

The most famous text, perhaps, in defense of *jihad* is Sura 9:5: "When the forbidden months are past, fight and slay the

---

[46]Firestone, "Conceptions of Holy War in Biblical and Qur'anic Tradition," 108–15.

idolaters wherever you find them, and seize them, beleaguer them, and lie in wait for them in every stratagem (of war); but if they repent and establish regular prayers and pay the alms tax, then open the way for them, for God is oft-forgiving, most merciful."[47] In light of full biblical teaching, one thing is clear: Whether Christian or Muslim, "holy war" has no justification and for that reason must be condemned. Only a flawed theology that fails to distinguish Yahweh war in its unique setting from any other kind of conflict can possibly defend its continuing, devastating consequences.

CONCLUSION

Basic to the problem of Yahweh war in the Old Testament, with its corollary application of *ḥerem* or genocide, is the nature of God, for it is he, according to the sacred text, who conceived, instigated, implemented, and benefited from it. But ultimate penetration of that nature is impossible, so one must rest content with the theological construct that God is holy, righteous, and just, but also gracious, merciful, and forgiving. These apparently mutually exclusive traits coexist in the record without resolution. Thus, the moral and ethical dilemma of Yahweh war must also remain without satisfying rational explanation. At the risk of cliché, all that can be said is that if God is all the Bible says he is, all that he does must be good—and that includes his authorization of genocide.

One must quickly reaffirm, however, that the genocide sanctioned by Scripture was unique to its time, place, and circumstances. It is not to be carried over to the age of the church. Indeed, it must remain an unused tool in the armory of a sovereign God until he comes in power and glory to establish his everlasting kingdom. He will then unleash his sword and, in a final and terrible display of his righteous wrath, will overcome all who resist his lordship. Only then will peace prevail and the making of war be consigned to an unremembered past.

---

[47]Cited in ibid., 111–12.

RESPONSES TO
EUGENE H. MERRILL

A RESPONSE TO
EUGENE H. MERRILL

C. S. Cowles

A former student shared with me the sad story of his father, a dedicated lay leader of an evangelical church, who in mid-life set out to read the Bible through for the first time. He was first surprised, then shocked, and finally outraged by the frequency and ferocity of divinely initiated and sanctioned violence in the Old Testament. About halfway through the book of Job, he shut his Bible never to open it again and has not set foot inside a church since.

That man's name is Legion. True, not all who have had a similar experience leave the church or abandon the faith, but many lose all disposition to read the Old Testament. This is not surprising, for as Eugene Merrill admits, "the narrative from Adam to the Chronicler is blood-soaked with murder and war." Then Merrill sets for himself a large and virtually impossible task: "to justify [Yahweh war, which includes Canaanite genocide] in light of the character of God as a whole."

We cannot pretend, as we read these genocidal "texts of terror," that Jesus has not come. In him we see the complete and undistorted "image of the invisible God" (Col. 1:15). Consequently, when we read the Old Testament through the prism of the revelation of God disclosed in Jesus, we find Merrill's defense of Moses' rationale for the destruction of the Canaanites untenable.

Canaanite genocide was a practical necessity. The justification most often cited in Deuteronomy and Joshua for annihilating

the Canaanites, and reiterated by Merrill, was the need to purge
the land of its idolatrous inhabitants lest the Israelites become
spiritually corrupt. The assumption was that the Israelites were
morally superior to the inhabitants of Canaan. Yet, if the
Israelites' forty years of desert wanderings proved anything, it
was that they were just as prone to idolatry, immorality, and
wickedness as their neighbors. Even if they had become a truly
holy people and had been successful in purging the land of all
Canaanite influence, they were still surrounded by idolatrous
nations with all the risks of exposure and corruption. This did in
fact occur many times in their subsequent history, with Solomon's importation of foreign wives—along with their idolatrous
practices—being only the most notorious.

The "sanitized land theory" presents an unflattering view
of Israel's God. It was a virtual admission that in free and open
competition with Canaanite religion, Yahweh worship would
lose out. So the only solution was to exterminate the competition.
In any case, the *herem* campaign utterly failed. The Canaanites
were decimated but not destroyed, idolatry was not eradicated,
and the Israelites were not preserved from moral and spiritual
pollution. What could be more morally bankrupting and spiritually corrupting than slaughtering men, women, and children?
The Canaanite holocaust stands in judgment on all attempts to
attain, maintain, and enforce holiness by coercive means.

Canaanite genocide projected God's sovereignty. Merrill
manifests a concern with "guarding" and "celebrating" Yahweh's sovereignty,, which is accomplished only through the
"total eradication" of "those who promote and practice the worship of false gods." This construal of Israel's God casts him in
the image of an insecure, tin-pot tyrant like Herod the Great,
whose paranoia drove him to eradicate all actual and imagined
competitors, including his wife Mariamne, three of his sons, and
all the male infants in Bethlehem.

Such a low view of God's sovereignty finds no correspondence whatsoever in Jesus. He cared so little about exercising his
sovereignty that even though he eternally existed "in [the] very
nature [of] God," he "made himself nothing" and took upon himself "the very nature of a servant" (Phil. 2:6–7). Jesus neither
threatened nor coerced compliance from anybody: not the rich
young ruler, not his wavering disciples, not the recalcitrant

Samaritans, not even Judas. Much less did he order the annihilation of the scribes, Pharisees, and chief priests along with their wives and children and all the inhabitants of their cities.

The God disclosed in Jesus is not an omnipotent enforcer who pursues his grand "hidden plan" (John Calvin) regardless of how many cities are destroyed and people are exterminated. His way of being in the world is not that of a genocidal despot but of a creative, life-giving, life-enhancing servant. He is omnipotent Lord, but his sovereignty is the sovereignty of self-emptying, cruciform love.

Canaanite genocide was part of God's salvation strategy. "The reason for [implementing Yahweh war] is clear," says Merrill. "Israel was the elect people of God, chosen not just to mediate the message of salvation to the world but also to serve as his agent in bringing to pass his will on the earth." What "message of salvation," we might ask, did the Canaanites hear as the Israelites were cutting them to pieces and burning them with fire? What were they to conclude about the character of Israel's God other than that he was more vicious, more cruel, and more merciless than Baal, Chemosh, Molech, or any of their gods? In destroying the Canaanites, the Israelites betrayed their own unique covenantal destiny as the ones through whom "all peoples on earth will be blessed" (Gen. 12:3). It fixed a dark blot on salvation history that lingers to this day.

Canaanite genocide displayed God's power and glory. "The pedagogical value of Yahweh war," says Merrill, "is that its display of God's power and wrath on the one hand, and of his grace and glory on the other, would lead both Israel and the nations of the earth to recognize his sovereignty." The biblical record clearly indicates otherwise. Rather than bringing "glory to God" as Moses anticipated, it so sullied, stained, profaned, distorted, and debased the image of God that God's name is "blasphemed among the Gentiles" (Rom. 2:24) to this day. Not a single nation was attracted to Israel's God, nor were they drawn to swear allegiance to Yahweh's sovereignty.

No psalms were composed celebrating the extermination of the Canaanites. No hymns extol the slaughter of the Amalekites. No holidays remember the Conquest. Jewish and Christian parents hide their children's eyes from *herem* passages. Pastors avoid it in preaching. Bible teachers dance around its intractable theological and moral problem. Canaanite genocide is a huge embarrassment to sensitive believers and an outrage to unbelievers.

Canaanite genocide was a righteous and holy act. "The fact that Israel alone was the elect nation charged with such astounding privilege and responsibility," says Merrill, "means that Israel alone could prosecute Yahweh war as a righteous act." What is this? The wanton slaughter of human beings—little children and tiny infants, fetuses in mother's wombs, the infirm and aged, the mentally retarded and physically handicapped, the blind and lame—was an "astounding privilege"? A "righteous act"? What, we wonder, might an "unrighteous act" look like? It is impossible to imagine ancient Israelites or modern-day Jews looking back on the killing of Canaanites as an "astounding privilege," much less that they would be thankful for being "elect" of God to introduce ḥerem ideology and practice into world history. If there has ever been an example of the genocidal sins of the fathers visited upon the children, it certainly has tragically been the case for the Jews.

Most incomprehensible of Merrill's many-faceted defense of "biblical genocide" is his claim that "the issue ... cannot be whether or not genocide is intrinsically good or evil—its sanction by a holy God settles that question." He goes on to assert that genocide is "in line with the character of God himself," that it "is not, for that reason, unjust or immoral," and that since "all that [God] does must be good ... that includes his authorization of genocide."

If the indiscriminate slaughter of human beings for any reason can be called a "good" and "righteous" act, and if the sanctity of human life established in creation, reaffirmed after the Flood, reinforced in the seventh commandment, reiterated by all the prophets, and incarnate in Jesus—if this can be set aside by a supposed divine "authorization of genocide"—then all moral and ethical absolutes are destroyed, all distinctions between good and evil are rendered meaningless, and all claims about God's love and compassion become cruel deceptions. It represents the ultimate corruption of human language and makes meaningful theological discourse virtually impossible.

What is missing in Merrill's ghastly portrait of the destroyer God is any mention of the *agapē* love that God has for "the world"—a love so great and all-encompassing that he "gave his one and only Son" (John 3:16). Lacking in all of this glorying in what the Geneva War Convention has labeled as "crimes against humanity" is any hint of a God who "wants all men to be saved and to come to a knowledge of the truth" (1 Tim. 2:4). That is hardly surprising, for genocide at any time, in any form, for any reason, is absolutely antithetical to love. It is alien to the nature of God who revealed himself in Jesus as "not wanting anyone to perish, but everyone to come to repentance" (2 Peter 3:9). It stands in total contradiction to everything that Jesus represented and taught, as Merrill candidly admits.[1]

Any theological construct, no matter how many biblical texts may be lined up in its support, that does not have the cross at its center is not only anti-Christ but dangerous. It opens wide the door for the very kinds of bloodshed and atrocities that have discredited the gospel in the past, and it gives biblical sanction to those who would twist God's Word to justify horrific acts of murder and mayhem in the present and future.

The church has, from New Testament times to the present, gloried in the good news that in Jesus, and Jesus alone, we have "'Immanuel'—which means, 'God with us'" (Matt. 1:23). For two thousand years, Christian orthodoxy has declared that the apostle John got it right when he categorically claimed that "God is love" (1 John 4:8, 16), that in Jesus and on his cross we see God's attitude toward sinners fully displayed, and that "whoever lives in love lives in God, and God in him" (4:16).

---

[1]"Jesus did not counsel violence, promote it in any way, or condone it when his followers were inclined otherwise."

A RESPONSE TO
EUGENE H. MERRILL

Daniel L. Gard

Eugene Merrill has provided a stimulating look at "Yahweh war" through the eyes of dispensationalism. I appreciate many of the points that he has made and the reverent manner in which he approaches the biblical books. While I would dissent from his millennialist reading of the eschatological texts, I do not do so by juxtaposing my own reading as "neutral" over and against his as "millennialist." In my opinion, it is impossible to read any text, including sacred Scripture, in a completely neutral manner. We all bring a set of presuppositions to the reading, formulated explicitly or implicitly around our own confessional principles. This is as true for those of us from the amillennialist school as from the various millennialistic traditions.

Nevertheless, both Merrill and I have reached the similar conclusion that it is improper for any nation to exercise genocide in the name of God against another nation. Only ancient Israel could do so, and then only when God commanded it. I would differ from Merrill not in that conclusion but in the implications of the conclusion for understanding God in past, present, and future.

Theology proper. As a starting point, we must begin with theology proper—that is, thinking and talking about God himself. Merrill makes an interesting proposal in stating that "God's holiness does not exist in a vacuum, as only an abstract quality. He is holy because he stands apart from that which is not; in fact, his holiness opposes everything and everyone that falls short of his perfection." Indeed, it is possible to speak of divine attributes as negative (imperfect characteristics found in human beings that cannot be ascribed to God) or positive (attributes found in human beings but that are ascribed to God in an absolute and higher degree).

Among the positive attributes of God is his holiness. This holiness, with which Merrill begins his discussion of the enemies of God, is not derived from comparisons to his creation. Before God created anything seen or unseen, he was holy. When he utterly destroys Satan and his minions on the last day and nothing evil remains with which to compare God, he will still be holy. That is because his holiness is inseparable from his essence.

With that said, the important question is not so much why certain nations were destroyed but rather why all nations, including Israel, were not. By Yahweh's standard of holiness, not even the most righteous of humanity could remain alive. Merrill states rightly that "those subject to Yahweh war were deserving of it, for their condition of rebellion—no matter how it came about—left no alternative." But here he does not draw out its implications. It is not only those who were subject to Yahweh war but all human beings who deserved annihilation, since by virtue of sin all stand in opposition to God's holiness.

Some other essential attribute of God must surely come into play here. That attribute (again, a positive attribute), I would suggest, is his love. Synonymous with his love is his mercy, grace, long-suffering, and patience. These are the attributes that sought and provided the salvation of the world. These are the attributes that spared Israel from total annihilation when their God warred against his own people. These are the attributes that are withholding the final Day of Judgment, in which all who oppose the holiness of Yahweh will face the great and final *herem*. Much more than "God's reputation and sovereignty" are at stake. Those attributes are above the ability of the most evil aspects of creation to comprehend, since they comprise the very nature of the Creator.

The continued existence of nations in rebellion cannot be explained from the basis of God's holiness, sovereignty, and reputation. Truly the exterminated nations opposing Israel deserved their fate. But so did all other nations then, and so do all nations today. Even Israel deserved the same fate. It is not only divine justice that is served in the warfare narratives; it is also divine mercy in that the human family is allowed to continue to exist.

Yahweh war. It is in this light that I would both agree and disagree with Merrill's four-point assessment of the reason for Yahweh war. It surely was necessary because of the hardness of heart of the enemy, for the protection of Israel, for the eradication of idolatry, and for the education of Israel and other nations. But more than this, it was for the preparation of the nation of Israel to bring forth the One who would come as a Savior not only for Israel but for all the children of Adam.

Before leaving this point, I would respectfully disagree with Merrill's assessment of what the "eradication of idolatry" implies. He states that "while theoretically heathenism can exist in the abstract, that is, apart from its proponents, in Israel's experience idolatry was linked to peoples and nations with whom she came in contact. This is why its removal was contingent on the destruction of those nations." I would suggest that false religion cannot exist in the abstract or apart from its proponents since the god they worship has no existence except in their imaginations. Whereas the true God is all things in and of himself (including, as above, "holiness"), idols are the construction of fallen humanity.

Idolatry went far beyond Israel's experience with other people; it arose also within Israel itself. For this reason, God sent prophets to warn his people and used foreign nations (e.g., Babylon) to chastise them without destroying them. Nevertheless, the destruction of nations did not produce the effect of removing idolatry. It continued on—even to this day.

Relationship between the Testaments. Merrill's work provides some interesting perspectives on the relationship between the Old and New Testaments. He states regarding the Olivet Discourse that "it is significant that Jesus makes no reference in this lengthy discourse to anything resembling Old Testament Yahweh war, though clearly he describes an age of incredible persecution and distress." However, earlier he had stated that "the retaliatory battle against Midian (Num. 31:1–24) is . . . clearly Yahweh war, though the technical language is largely missing." If this is so for Numbers 31:1–24, and I do not disagree that it is, then it can also be so for the Olivet Discourse. Further illuminating the "Yahweh-war" images of Jesus' eschatological teaching are the language and imagery of the intertestamental literature, which permeate New Testament apocalyptic imagery. The words of Jesus cannot, in my opinion, speak of anything but the final and cataclysmic holy war with its great and final *ḥerem*.

Earlier I stated that I do not believe it is possible to have a completely neutral reading of a biblical text. Eugene Merrill has provided an example of this, against which I would offer my own equally preinformed reading. In his interpretation of "Yahweh War and the New Testament," Merrill provides a classic millennialist reading of the end times. He takes the book of Revelation as a work filled with apocalyptic symbols. With this I fully concur, since the canonical Apocalypse shares much language and imagery with other literature of the genre. However, it is interesting that the Apocalypse's reference to a thousand years, set in the midst of what is mutually agreed to be symbolic language, is taken literally. Should it not be taken symbolically, just as the other language of the book is properly understood?

This question, of course, reflects the fundamentally different hermeneutics of millennialism and amillennialism. I do not pretend to be able to resolve that issue here. Readers can appreciate the clear explication of the texts in question utilizing a particular set of interpretive principles with which they may happen to disagree.

Ethical issues. Interestingly, however, I find myself in agreement with Merrill's conclusions regarding the ethical issues set before the Christian. He clearly concludes that the Christian cannot be guided "by the Old Testament principles and practices of Yahweh war." Quite rightly, he asserts that these principles applied only to "the Israelite theocracy."

Merrill further warns against Christian appeals to eschatological texts. I fully agree with this, although for quite different reasons. In my view, these texts apply not to "a regathered Israel" or to a millennial age. Rather, they apply to the last day, that instant in which time ends and Jesus returns with his angels as the great and final Judge. In this case, two differing eschatological systems (millennialist and amillennialist) meet in agreement regarding the ethics of believers who await Christ's return.

I thank Dr. Eugene Merrill for an outstanding contribution to this topic. Although I disagree with him in certain places theologically and hermeneutically, I am appreciative of the perspective he has brought to a difficult issue.

A RESPONSE TO
EUGENE H. MERRILL

Tremper Longman III

Eugene Merrill's essay is characterized by his usual exegetical care and precision. He also synthesizes the exegetical material well, showing his insight as a theologian. Indeed, I believe that there is not a large difference between the perspective argued by Dr. Merrill and my own. This is perhaps illustrative of the fact that the theological divide between dispensationalists, the tradition of Merrill (who teaches at Dallas Theological Seminary), and covenant theology, which I represent, is not as large as it used to be. In part, this is because many dispensationalists now recognize that there is considerable continuity between the Testaments, while many covenant theologians, like Meredith Kline and myself, are willing to see the discontinuities. Certainly there continue to be differences—and there are hardliners on both sides—but on this particular topic Dr. Merrill and I have considerable agreement.

In particular, I was impressed with and learned from Merrill's reflections on the relationship between the covenant and holy war. I want to think further about it before offering my wholesale agreement, but there seems to be considerable truth to his statement that

> it was only after Israel had been constituted as a nation
> following that revelation that Yahweh war became not
> just a display of God's redemptive power and grace on
> behalf of his people but a constituent part of the covenant

relationship itself. Israel from then on would not just witness God's mighty deeds as heavenly warrior but would be engaged in bringing them to pass.

I also found interesting and important his comments about Yahweh war being in the first place wars against pagan nations' "imaginary gods." However, it may be going too far to suggest that these wars are "deicide rather than homicide." After all, a lot of human beings were killed. It does not seem that Merrill uses this as an easy escape from the ethical problem of the Old Testament. Rather, he admirably grounds his justification of God's participation in war in his "omnipotence, his infinite wisdom, and, above all, his holiness." He does this in a way that does not divorce these attributes from God's "love, grace, mercy, and forbearance."

Even so, I was not always comfortable when Merrill provided what I thought was too neat an explanation for why the Canaanites were the object of God's warring wrath in a way that, say, the Egyptians were not. I am not in total disagreement with him because he rightly points to some passages that talk about the special sin of the Canaanites and even, in the case of Genesis 15:16, God's patience with them. Moreover, the understanding of the Canaanites as squatters on land that was not theirs may in one sense be correct, but certainly the Canaanites had no clue that this was the case. With all our appropriate attempts to try to justify God's violence toward the Canaanites, I think that ultimately we simply have to appeal to God's wisdom, holiness, and omnipotence (as Merrill indeed suggested in another place). To us, his human creatures, God the warrior is a mystery, and, as Isaiah 28:21 describes, his temporal judgment is a "strange work"[1]:

> The LORD will rise up as he did at Mount Perazim,
>   he will rouse himself as in the Valley of Gibeon—
> to do his work, his strange work,
>   and perform his task, his alien task.

I would also question, or at least nuance, Merrill's unit on "Israel: The Divine Instrument." I think he gives the wrong

---

[1]In this regard, the book of Job may be relevant here. Job discusses suffering but leaves the reader without an explanation of suffering. Instead, the reader, like Job, is invited to submit before a mysterious deity.

impression when he says, "Israel's role in the implementation of Yahweh war needs careful attention because *only Israel was authorized to carry it out in Old Testament times*" (emphasis original). Is this strictly true? After all, Jeremiah announces that God the warrior will be at the head of the Babylonian army in the destruction of covenant-breaking Israel (Jer. 21:3–7). Daniel sees the hand of God behind Nebuchadnezzar's earlier siege of Jerusalem (Dan. 1:1–3). Isaiah even calls Cyrus the messiah, God's anointed one, because he will lead an army against the oppressive Babylonians (cf. Isa. 45:1–7).

If I am right about this, then one of Merrill's main arguments against modern holy war (a position I agree with but provide other arguments to support) are too weak. He writes: "If no case could be made for Yahweh war without Israel's participation in Old Testament times, surely none can be made today whether done in the name of Christ, Allah, or any other authority."

Despite these disagreements, Merrill and I agree on much. He rightly argues that the Old Testament texts do not justify Yahweh war today except in terms of spiritual conflict (my phase 4), though I wish he had explicated the nature of the spiritual conflict and had tied it in explicitly with Old Testament physical battles, as I tried to do. And, as opposed to Cowles, he brings eschatology into view here as well and recognizes that the Christ who returns will be a judging, warring figure (Rev. 19:11–21). True, as we get into the details of the interpretation of certain apocalyptic passages, we might disagree over whether they are metaphoric or literal, but we both recognize the possibility of both.

Chapter Three

THE CASE FOR
ESCHATOLOGICAL CONTINUITY

Daniel L. Gard

THE CASE FOR
ESCHATOLOGICAL CONTINUITY

Daniel L. Gard

Genocide. The systematic slaughter of a group or race of people—or a nation. In 1945, the world reacted with horror as the evidence of Nazi atrocities against Jews, Gypsies, and others mounted. In more recent years, the world watched in real time on network news channels as the horrors of genocide in Rwanda and the Balkans became known. As these slipped from the collective memory of the public, four airplanes were hijacked on September 11, 2001, and three of them successfully crashed into buildings, resulting in the loss of thousands of lives. The hatred within the terrorists and their particular understanding of the Islamic teaching on *jihad* (known to most English-speaking people as "holy war") again brings genocide to the foreground. In the name of religion, a blow was struck announcing the intention to kill a people (Americans) wherever they might be.

Against this contemporary background, readers of the Old Testament are confronted with the startling account of genocide by Israel at the command of Yahweh their God. The violence of these scenes is (for the Christian reader) in stark contrast to the image of Jesus as the kind, good, and gentle Shepherd. Instead of these pastoral images, God appears in many Old Testament texts as the divine warrior at whose command nations are destroyed. Nevertheless, people like the Ku Klux Klan have embraced the Old Testament warfare narratives and used them to justify their violence against blacks, Jews, and others.

113

This presents a moral dilemma for Christian readers of the Old Testament. How should we read and apply the Old Testament? How could a God of love, known in the pages of the New Testament as the meek and gentle Lamb of God, command such brutal practices? Should a wedge be placed between the Old and New Testaments in order to preserve the integrity of both? Can there be a connection between these ancient accounts of God's people (Israel) and the image of God as Savior so prevalent in the Gospels?

Few would react as did the second-century theologian Marcion, whose dualism construed the God of the Old Testament to be an inferior God to that of the New Testament. Nevertheless, can the genocide of the Old Testament serve as warrant for the modern genocide of those deemed to be enemies of God?

Some scholars answer these questions by reading the Old Testament accounts of warfare and genocide and rejecting them out of hand as having any valid history. To them, these writings are little more than theological writings of (much) later generations recording the legends and myths of their people. Thus, they are of more use in analyzing the time in which the books were written down than in establishing either history or theology. Evangelical scholars like myself, however, have to deal with these questions because we maintain that these accounts reflect historical events and are not merely the later reflections of Israel. Revelation takes place not only through the written Scripture but also through the acts of God in history. Thus, even in the brutality of ancient warfare, God reveals himself.

As time went on, however, the warfare narratives of the earliest books of the Old Testament did receive a transformation in their theological function. One stage in this development is apparent in 1 and 2 Chronicles, which come so late in the Old Testament canon that they provide a gateway to the intertestamental period and to the New Testament. A trajectory can be developed that leads from the earliest narratives of the Old Testament, to the warfare narratives of Chronicles, to the intertestamental apocalypses, and to the images of the victorious Christ in John's Revelation. It is this trajectory that enables us to deal with the questions posed above.

My approach is based on several assumptions. (1) For many reasons (including my a priori creedal assertion) I maintain that the Scripture is reliable as a historical text. (2) Old Testament texts, including the genocide texts, must be read in their canonical context of both Old and New Testaments. (3) The events of the Old Testament may serve as types of that which is to come in the New Testament or, at a minimum, provide the imagery used by New Testament authors. (4) The Scriptures speak of things yet to be, including the eschatological hope of Christ's return and the founding of a new heaven and new earth.

It is through an eschatological reading of warfare narratives—including their accounts of divinely mandated genocide—that the images of Old Testament genocide can be seen as types of an eschatological event. I will take several steps to demonstrate this. (1) I will examine the "ban," or *herem*, as a part of "holy war" during which biblical incidents of genocide occurred. (2) I will then examine five elements illustrating the consistent holy-war tradition in both early and late Old Testament texts as the baseline from which later texts diverge. (3) Next, I will describe a trajectory from the end of the Old Testament through the intertestamental period to the New Testament. (4) Finally, I will describe the continuity between the Old and New Testaments in light of the genocide texts as an eschatological continuity.

THE CONTEXT OF GENOCIDE IN THE OLD TESTAMENT AND MODERN SCHOLARSHIP

The twentieth-century German scholar Gerhard von Rad observed a series of thirteen characteristics of "holy war" in various Old Testament texts.[1] Of these characteristics, perhaps the

---

[1]Gerhard von Rad, *Der heilige Krieg im alten Israel*, 4th ed. (Göttingen: Vandenhoeck & Ruprecht, 1965). Here they are:

1. the blowing of a trumpet as the announcement of the holy war (Judg. 3:27; 6:34–35; 1 Sam. 13:3)
2. the naming of the army as the "people of Yahweh" (Judg. 5:11, 13; 20:2)
3. the sanctification of the participants (Num. 21:2; Deut. 23:9–14; Josh. 3:5; Judg. 11:36; 1 Sam. 14:24; 21:5; 2 Sam. 1:21; 11:11–12)
4. the sacrificing of an offering and/or the consultation of Yahweh (Judg. 20:23, 26, 27; 1 Sam. 7:9; 13:9–10, 12; 14:8–9; 2 Sam. 5:19, 23)
5. the announcement of victory by Yahweh, "I have given ... into your hand," or similar phraseology (Josh. 2:24; 6:2, 16; 8:1, 18; 10:8, 19; Judg. 3:28; 4:7, 14; 7:9, 15; 18:10; 20:28; 1 Sam. 14:12; 17:46; 23:4; 24:5; 26:8; 1 Kings 20:28)

(list continues on following page)

most shocking to modern readers is the twelfth, the practice of the ban or *ḥerem*. This practice amounts to genocide committed by Israel at the command of their God. Further, it was a part of Israel's warfare as literally as any other characteristic.

In its purest form, the *ḥerem* in warfare refers to the devotion of all spoils to Yahweh and the destruction of all life (Josh. 6:17–21; 7:11–15). Inflammable objects were to be burned (Deut. 7:25–26), but noncombustible precious metals were to be taken to the sanctuary treasury (Josh. 6:24). It was forbidden to spare any person alive who was under the *ḥerem*. In some cases, the *ḥerem* was partially eased by the exemption of women and children (Num. 31:7–12, 17–18; Deut. 20:13–14; 21:10–14) and, in particular, the young virgin women (Judg. 21:11–21). A point of tension exists on the issue of cattle; according to Deuteronomy 2:34–35, they could be saved, but 1 Samuel 15:9, 21 demanded their destruction. In the matter of the people of the land, however, there was no equivocation: The Hittites, the Amorites, the Canaanites, the Perizzites, the Hivites, and the Jebusites were to be utterly destroyed so that nothing that breathed should live (Deut. 20:16–18).

In understanding this practice, it is important to realize that the nation of Israel was not unique here in the ancient Near East. They were following the practices of other nations, which prac-

---

6. the announcement that Yahweh goes out before the army (Deut. 20:4; Josh. 3:11; Judg. 4:14; 2 Sam. 5:24)

7. the claiming of the war as "Yahweh's war" and the enemy as "Yahweh's enemy" (Ex. 14:4, 14, 18; Deut. 1:30; Josh. 10:14, 42; 11:6; 23:10; Judg. 20:35; 1 Sam. 14:23)

8. the encouragement not to fear because the enemy will lose courage (Ex. 14:13; Deut. 20:3; Josh. 8:1; 10:8, 25; 11:6; Judg. 7:3; 1 Sam. 23:16–17; 30:6; 2 Sam. 10:12)

9. the fear of Yahweh among enemy troops (Ex. 15:14–16; 23:27–28; Lev. 26:36; Deut. 2:25; 11:25; Josh. 2:9, 24; 5:1; 7:5; 10:2; 11:20; 24:12; 1 Sam. 4:7–8; 17:11; 28:5)

10. the war-shout (Josh. 6:5; Judg. 7:20; 1 Sam. 17:20, 52)

11. the intervention of Yahweh, who strikes terror into the hearts of the enemy (Ex. 23:27; Deut. 7:23; Josh. 10:10–11; 24:7; Judg. 4:15; 7:22; 1 Sam. 5:11; 7:10; 14:15, 20)

12. the practice of the "ban" (*ḥerem*), the slaughter of all enemy men, women, and children (Num. 21:2; Josh. 6:18–19; 1 Sam. 15)

13. the dismissal of the troops with the cry, "To your tents, O Israel" (2 Sam. 20:1; 1 Kings 12:16; 22:36)

ticed their own equivalent of *ḥerem*. The term itself is used by at least one other nation, Moab, as found in the Moabite Mesha[2] Stela:

> Chemosh spoke to me: Go, take Nebo from Israel! Then (15) I went by night and fought ... against it [Nebo] from day-break to noon. And (16) I took it ... and totally destroyed it ...: 7,000 citizens and aliens, male and female (17) together with female slaves; for I had consecrated it to Ashtar-Chemosh for destruction [... *hḥrmth*]. Then I took ... thence the (18) vessels of Yahweh and brought them before Chemosh.[3]

A second text from Mesha's campaign has also been seen as an imposition of *ḥerem* against the Israelite population of Ataroth:[4]

> I killed all the people from (?) (12) the city as a *ryt* (delight, satisfaction, propitiatory sacrifice?) for Chemosh and for Moab.[5]

The term *ryt*, likely a sacrificial term, implies a consecration to deity; thus, "consecration to destruction during a war of conquest was thought of in ninth-century Moab as a sacrifice to the deity."[6] Terminology such as "a man devotes to Yahweh [*yhrm ʾyš lyhwh*]" (Lev. 27:28; cf. Mic. 4:13) and "shall be devoted ... to Yahweh [*hrm ... lyhwh*]" (Josh. 6:17) bear a close resemblance to the usage at Moab.

Still another term, *asakkum*, appears in the cuneiform texts of Mari from the eighteenth century B.C.[7] In these texts the phrase "to eat the *asakkum*" of gods or the king indicates a violation of a decree regarding the spoils of war. At Mari, unlike Israel or Moab,

---

[2]Mesha, a king of Moab who rebelled against Israel in the ninth century B.C. (2 Kings 3), boasts of placing the *ḥerem* on the Israelites (Pritchard, *ANET*, 320).

[3]Translated by N. Lohfink (see "חָרַם," *TDOT*, 5:189). However, according to Lohfink, because the sentence in question is an inverted summary clause that interrupts a series of prefix clauses, it is questionable whether the verb *hrm* "refers here not to the actual destruction of the populace but to their preceding consecration to destruction" (5:189–90).

[4]J. Liver, "The Wars of Mesha, King of Moab," *PEQ* 99 (1967): 24–31.

[5]Translated by Lohfink, "חָרַם," 5:190.

[6]Ibid. Lohfink, however, questions whether this is an instance of *hrm* since the term is not used.

[7]Abraham Malamat, "The Ban in Mari and the Bible," in *Mari and the Bible* (Jerusalem: Hebrew Univ. Press, 1975), 52–61.

asakkum was only temporary, so that booty could be distributed later. Further, *asakkum* did not involve the total destruction of the population of conquered cities. Although the range of meaning of Israel's term *ḥerem* clearly exceeded the semantic range of *asakkum* at Mari,[8] a close connection can be seen between the fate of captured cities/populations and their consecration to deity.

By postexilic times, the verb *ḥrm* was used with different connotations in the biblical texts. In Ezra 10:8, those who refused to participate in the Jerusalem assembly were subject to *ḥerem*. Here the term refers not to destruction of person or property but to the confiscation of the nonparticipant's property for the temple treasury.[9] However, in the context of warfare narratives in the postexilic era, *ḥrm* continued to mean the destruction of things devoted to Yahweh.[10]

It is important to remember that the ban or *ḥerem* is only one aspect of ancient "holy war" and must be placed in the context of how Israel understood its warfare in general. Though popularized by Gerhard von Rad,[11] the expression "holy war" is not found in the text of Scripture itself, although the concept is certainly deeply rooted in the biblical tradition. While the specific term has not found universal scholarly acceptance,[12] it remains useful as a technical term for the phenomenon described by von Rad.

Von Rad's work has profoundly affected the way in which many read the Old Testament warfare narratives. He drew a

---

[8]A. E. Glock, "Warfare in Mari and Early Israel" (Ph.D. diss., University of Michigan; available through University Microfilms, Ann Arbor, Mich., 1968).

[9]Joseph Blenkinsopp, *Ezra-Nehemiah: A Commentary* (OTL; Philadelphia: Westminster, 1988).

[10]The Chronicler uses the verb *ḥrm* and its cognates four times: 1 Chron. 2:7; 4:41; 2 Chron. 20:23; 32:14.

[11]Von Rad, *Der heilige Krieg im alten Israel*. Von Rad's use of the term and the reconstruction of holy war as the product of late theological reinterpretation of history can be traced to the earlier work of Friedrich Schwally, *Der heilige Krieg im alten Israel* (Leipzig: Dietrich, 1901).

[12]Some scholars have argued in favor of the term "Yahweh War" rather than "holy war," since the former is a biblical term while the latter is drawn from Greek usage. See, e.g., Gwilym H. Jones, "'Holy War' or 'Yahweh War'?" *VT* 25 (1965): 654–58; Rudolph Smend, *Yahweh War and Tribal Confederation*, trans. Max Gray Rogers (New York: Abingdon, 1970), 36–37; Manfred Weippert, "'Heiliger Krieg' in Israel und Assyrien: Kritische Anmerkungen zu Gerhard von Rads Konzept des 'Heiligen Kriegs im alten Israel'," *ZAW* 84 (1972): 460–93.

sharp distinction between holy war as a literary theological concept and whatever factual history that might lie behind the relevant narratives.[13] In his thinking, holy war was essentially a political and military institution—part of a sacral-cultic institution in Israel and thus primarily defensive in character. It is this aspect of von Rad's work that formed the primary point of departure for subsequent scholarship.

Two separate schools of thought emerged among those scholars who, since von Rad, have reflected on Israel's warfare.[14] Some scholars, like von Rad, understand holy war as the product of late theological history writing.[15] Other scholars believe that there are older historical events that are reflected in the text.[16] My own study of warfare would certainly place me in the latter camp, although I do not believe that most modern scholarship

---

[13]Von Rad (*Der heilige Krieg*, 18) dated Israel's holy-war episodes as no earlier than the period of the judges and as institutionally connected with the ancient amphictyony.

[14]A third group might include the reflections of ethicists and scholars from pacifist Christian traditions. Included among these are Patrick D. Miller Jr., "God the Warrior: A Problem in Biblical Interpretation and Apologetics," *Int* 19 (1965): 39–46; Waldemar Janzen, "War in the Old Testament," *Mennonite Quarterly Review* 46 (1972): 155–66; Jacob J. Enz, *The Christian and Warfare: The Roots of Pacifism in the Old Testament* (Scottdale, Pa.: Herald, 1972); John Howard Yoder, *The Politics of Jesus* (Grand Rapids: Eerdmans, 1972) and *The Original Revolution* (Scottdale, Pa.: Herald, 1972); Vernard Eller, *War and Peace from Genesis to Revelation* (Scottdale, Pa.: Herald, 1981). One monograph deserving special mention is that of Millard C. Lind, *Yahweh Is a Warrior* (Scottdale, Pa.: Herald, 1980). Writing from the perspective of one of the traditional "peace churches," Lind argues that the theology of Yahweh as warrior centers on three major emphases. (1) The Exodus provides the fundamental paradigm of divine intervention through a miracle of nature rather than ordinary human warfare. The central human figure here is not a warrior but a prophetic figure (Moses). (2) The prophetic political structure of Israel rejected kingship grounded in violence with the king as representative of divinity. (3) Yahweh warred against Israel when it became like other Near Eastern states.

[15]For example, Schwally, *Der heilige Krieg im alten Israel*; Patrick D. Miller Jr., *The Divine Warrior in Early Israel* (HSM 5; Cambridge, Mass.: Harvard Univ. Press, 1973); Weippert, "'Heiliger Krieg' in Israel und Assyrien."

[16]Fritz Stolz, *Jahwes und Israels Krieg: Kriegstheorien und Kriegserfahrungen im Glaube des alten Israels*; Roland de Vaux, *Ancient Israel*, 2 vols. (New York: McGraw-Hill, 1965), 1:213–66; Smend, *Yahweh War and Tribal Confederation*; E. W. Conrad, *Fear Not Warrior: A Study of the 'al tîrā' Pericopes in the Hebrew Scriptures* (BJS 75; Chico, Calif.: Scholars Press, 1985); T. R. Hobbs, *A Time for War: A Study of Warfare in the Old Testament* (Wilmington, Del.: Michael Glazier, 1989).

adequately recognizes the theological, canonical, and historical context of Israel's warfare.

In summary, the biblical text reflects the historical practice of warfare and genocide in the ancient Near East. *Herem* was not uniquely an Israelite practice insofar as others also engaged in the destruction and consecration of their enemies to their gods.

THE BASELINE: COMMONALITY IN THE EARLY AND LATER OLD TESTAMENT TEXTS

The simplest way to develop the trajectory from the earliest warfare narratives through to the end of the Old Testament, through the intertestamental period, and on into the New Testament is to trace particular themes in which there is a large degree of consistency. Thus, I will draw here a baseline of five themes of the warfare context of genocide from the early Old Testament period to the late Old Testament period: (1) the meaning of defeat; (2) the application of the law of war; (3) holy war as synergism or monergism; (4) the spoils of war; and (5) the holiness of the camp.

The Meaning of Defeat

What happens when Yahweh wars against his own people? The Hebrew Bible's record of God's activity in war is not limited to those instances where Yahweh fought for or alongside of Israel. Warfare was a mark of divine retribution. When Judah was defeated, images of a "reverse holy war" can be seen.

Biblical literature reflects on the meaning of defeat. Not only did the later prophets speak of its meaning both for Israel and for other nations, but the earlier texts addressed this problem as well. Numbers 14:41–45, for example, explains the defeat at Kadesh Barnea as the result of Yahweh's desertion of Israel:

> But Moses said, "Why are you disobeying the LORD's command? This will not succeed! Do not go up, because the LORD is not with you. You will be defeated by your enemies, for the Amalekites and Canaanites will face you there. Because you have turned away from the LORD, he will not be with you and you will fall by the sword."

Nevertheless, in their presumption they went up toward the high hill country, though neither Moses nor the ark of the LORD's covenant moved from the camp. Then the Amalekites and Canaanites who lived in that hill country came down and attacked them and beat them down all the way to Hormah.

Likewise, Joshua 7 explains Israel's defeat at Ai as the result of Yahweh's giving Israel into the hands of their enemy, because they did not destroy (*ḥrm*) the devoted things. And 1 Samuel 4:2–3a explains Israel's defeat by Philistia as the result of Yahweh bringing that defeat:

The Philistines deployed their forces to meet Israel, and as the battle spread, Israel was defeated by the Philistines, who killed about four thousand of them on the battlefield. When the soldiers returned to camp, the elders of Israel asked, "Why did the LORD bring defeat upon us today before the Philistines?"

Israel was defeated because their God had decreed and brought about that defeat.

The idea of a god fighting against his own people is also found in nonbiblical texts. Millard Lind cites, as the most comprehensive example, a Sumerian text that seeks to explain why the Guti could defeat the kingdom of Akkad. According to this document,[17] the fourth ruler of Akkad, Naram-Sin, had sacked Nippur, the city of Enlil, and desecrated his temple, Ekur. In revenge for Naram-Sin's actions, Enlil brought the Guti, a barbarous people, upon Akkad. Other gods, eight altogether, forsook Akkad in solidarity with Enlil:

She who had lived there, left the city, Like a maiden forsaking her chamber, Holy Inanna forsook the shrine Agade, Like a warrior hastening to (his) weapon, She went forth against the city in battle (and) combat, She attacked as if it were a foe.[18]

The Chronicler too cites various incidents as divine retribution against Israel, in line with the early biblical accounts and

---

[17]Millard Lind (*Yahweh Is a Warrior* [Scottsdale, Pa.: Herald, 1980], 111) summarizes the document's understanding of the relationship between gods and humans.
[18]*ANET*, 648.

the Sumerian text. Deity is offended at a cultic impropriety, the god fights against his or her people, and a foreign people become the instruments of destruction at the god's command.

But there are also important differences in Chronicles. In the Chronicler's narratives of defeat, the defeat is not postponed to later generations. Rather, it falls on the generation that has offended Yahweh. Most importantly, there remained for Judah a hope for the future; Akkad, by contrast, was destroyed without such hope. Even though Judah was destroyed finally by the Babylonians, that hope for the future was never destroyed.

The Chronicler takes narratives of Yahweh's war against his own people and explicates their theological meaning. Human armies do not determine the result of war. Only the God of Israel does that. History is always in his hands. Time after time, a superior Judah was defeated by an inferior army. Joash, who successfully bought off the Syrian invaders in 2 Kings 12:17–18, was defeated and killed by divine intervention in 2 Chronicles 24:24:

> Although the Aramean army had come with only a few men, the LORD delivered into their hands a much larger army. Because Judah had forsaken the LORD, the God of their fathers, judgment was executed on Joash.

The Chronicler's explanation of the defeat of Ahaz by Syria (Aram) and Ahaz's defeat by Assyria, the Edomites, and the Philistines is similar:

> Therefore the LORD his God handed him over to the king of Aram. The Arameans defeated him and took many of his people as prisoners and brought them to Damascus. He was also given into the hands of the king of Israel, who inflicted heavy casualties on him. (2 Chron. 28:5)

> The LORD had humbled Judah because of Ahaz king of Israel, for he had promoted wickedness in Judah and had been most unfaithful to the LORD. (2 Chron. 28:19)

Defeat in warfare is often explained as the result of Yahweh's judgment on the faithlessness of the king and people. Yahweh either sides with his faithful king and people, or he fights against his unfaithful king and people. Saul died in battle, according to the Chronicler, because he was unfaithful to Yahweh:

> Saul died because he was unfaithful to the LORD; he did
> not keep the word of the LORD and even consulted a
> medium for guidance, and did not inquire of the LORD.
> So the LORD put him to death and turned the kingdom
> over to David son of Jesse. (1 Chron. 10:13–14)

Unfaithful Ahaziah, through his alliance with Joram of Israel, was defeated and killed because "God brought about Ahaziah's downfall" (2 Chron. 22:7). The same explanation is given for Manasseh's defeat and captivity at the hands of the king of Assyria:

> So the LORD brought against them the army commanders
> of the king of Assyria, who took Manasseh prisoner, put
> a hook in his nose, bound him with bronze shackles and
> took him to Babylon. (2 Chron. 33:11)

The Exile itself is explained as occurring because Yahweh directed it: "He brought up against them the king of the Babylonians" (2 Chron. 36:17). This too occurred because the people had been unfaithful.

In each case, the Chronicler explains the defeat of Judah as occurring through the will of Yahweh. Whereas Yahweh elsewhere obtained victory on behalf of his faithful king and people, here Yahweh brought defeat. Enemy armies, regardless of their size compared to Judahite armies, could not win if Yahweh fought for his people. Nor could they lose if Yahweh fought against his people. The kings of the nations and the military machines they commanded were but instruments in the hands of Judah's God.

But let us note that the people of Israel were never totally destroyed. They were not subject to the complete annihilation of genocide. There always remained a remnant. For Israel, the warfare of Yahweh against his own people was never to destroy utterly, but to chasten and restore. Yahweh never imposed the "ban" or *ḥerem* against Israel in its fullest sense.

Application of the Law of War

From its founding as a nation, Israel engaged in warfare with its neighbors. The book of Deuteronomy provides a basic starting point from which the wars of Israel can be understood.

Deuteronomy 20 (along with 21; 23; 24; and 25) forms the basis for all later interpretation of warfare because these passages contain a series of six topics[19] related to how Israel was to conduct its warfare. Several specific examples of the laws of warfare can illustrate their ongoing significance for Israel into the later Old Testament period of the Chronicler. In Deuteronomy 20:2, for example, a prebattle speech had to be given by a priest. In 2 Chronicles 20:5–7, Jehoshaphat, in his role as a Davidic king, assumed the speech-making role designated for a priest. But the point of the speech was the same: God was with the army and would give victory.

The laws of war in Deuteronomy also anticipate an enemy force much larger than that of Israel. Deuteronomy 20:1 states: "When you go to war against your enemies and see horses and chariots and an army greater than yours, do not be afraid of them, because the LORD your God, who brought you up out of Egypt, will be with you." Second Chronicles 13:3 describes precisely this situation. Jeroboam's army of 800,000 marched against Abijah's comparatively small army of 400,000.[20] The war laws of Deuteronomy 20:4 assured Judah that Yahweh would fight for them against their enemies: "For the LORD your God is the one who goes with you to fight for you against your enemies to give you victory." This is echoed in Abijah's battle with Jeroboam. God defeated the northern kingdom (2 Chron. 13:15); all that was left for the army of Judah to do was pursue the enemy and slaughter them.

Another element of war in Deuteronomy 20:10 makes provision for offering peace terms to a besieged city: "When you march up to attack a city, make its people an offer of peace." Two possible responses are anticipated. The city may accept the peace terms and its inhabitants would then be conscripted as forced labor (20:11). Alternatively, they may refuse the peace offer, in which case Yahweh would give them into Israel's hand. All the men would be killed, but the women, children, and cattle would

---

[19]Gerhard von Rad, "Deuteronomy and the Holy War," in *Studies in Deuteronomy*, trans. David Stalker (London: SCM, 1953), 50–51. The six are: (1) laws concerning war (20:1–9); (2) investment of cities (20:10–18); (3) female prisoners of war (21:10–14); (4) the law concerning the camp (23:10–14); (5) exemption for the newly married (24:5); and (6) the law concerning Amalek (25:17–19).

[20]Judah faces exactly the same situation in two other warfare texts unique to the Chronicler (see 2 Chron. 14:8–9; 20:2). Further, the implications of 2 Chron. 12:2–3 and Shishak's invading army are much the same.

be spared and the inanimate booty taken by the Israelites for themselves. In the case of the people of the land, every living thing was to be destroyed (20:12–18). In Abijah's battle in 2 Chronicles 13, the long speech by Abijah offered peace terms to the northern kingdom: "Men of Israel, do not fight against the LORD, the God of your fathers, for you will not succeed" (2 Chron. 13:12). When the offer of peace was rejected, Abijah and his army killed 500,000 Israelite troops, taking cities and territory from Israel (13:17–19).

This point of comparison is the most significant for our purposes. The imposition of *herem* was not made against Israel. Even in defeat, the rebellious northern tribes were not treated in the same way that foreign enemies were treated. Although 500,000 of the 800,000 northern troops were killed, there yet remained a remnant of 300,000. Yahweh would not forget his covenant with the descendants of Abraham, even if Israel forgot it.

Holy War As Synergism or Monergism

A third theme of the trajectory focuses on the question of whether Yahweh fights *for* or *with* his people. In other words, is Yahweh's war monergistic or synergistic?

In some cases, Yahweh fought unaided by Israel. In two of the earliest poems of the Hebrew Bible,[21] the victory of Yahweh as sole warrior is celebrated. Both the Song of Miriam (15:21) and the Song of the Sea (15:1–18) exult in Yahweh's victory:

> I will sing to the LORD,
>   for he is highly exalted.
> The horse and its rider
>   he has hurled into the sea.
> The LORD is my strength and my song;
>   he has become my salvation.
> He is my God, and I will praise him,
>   my father's God, and I will exalt him.
> The LORD is a warrior;
>   the LORD is his name. (Ex. 15:1–3)

---

[21]Lind (*Yahweh Is a Warrior*, 46) has argued that the Exodus and desert period is the Hebrew Bible's time of holy war par excellence, contra von Rad (*Der heilige Krieg im alten Israel*; the period of the judges) and Miller (*The Divine Warrior in Early Israel*; the period of the Conquest).

Throughout the song, there is no hint of human participation in the battle. Yahweh alone did battle. As the poem relates the events of Yahweh's victory, it was the victory of Yahweh the king: "The LORD will reign for ever and ever" (Ex. 15:18). Similarly, in 2 Chronicles 32, Yahweh alone did battle during the invasion of Hezekiah's Judah by Sennacherib. No action was performed in battle by the people; rather, the angel of Yahweh "annihilated all the fighting men and the leaders and officers in the camp of the Assyrian king" (32:21).[22]

Battles in which Yahweh was the sole actor on behalf of his people stand in contrast to other biblical and nonbiblical ancient Near Eastern warfare narratives. In some cases, the god fought unaided, as in the Baal epic and Baal's defeat of Yam.[23] Normally, however, there was a degree of cooperation between human and deity. Illustrative of this are the ninth-century Mesopotamian reliefs of Ashurnasirpal II,[24] shown in battle with the image of Ashur above him and with both king and god drawing bows. In a second relief, both Ashurnasirpal II and the god Ashur are shown in a victory parade with slung bow.

The image of Yahweh fighting in cooperation with his people is a common motif in the Hebrew Bible as well. A poem of about the same age as the Song of the Sea is the Song of Deborah (Judg. 5:1–31). This song, unlike Exodus 15, speaks of a cooperation on the part of the people, who joined Yahweh in battle against the northern Canaanite cities: "When the princes in Israel take the lead, when the people willingly offer themselves—praise the LORD!" (Judg. 5:2). Both Yahweh (5:3–5, 19–21, 28, 31) and the people fought (5:2, 6–18, 22–27, 29–30).

The two motifs of Yahweh fighting alone and Yahweh fighting in conjunction with the people are interwoven in the biblical warfare narratives. In some texts from the postexilic Chronicles, the primary actors are the human actors. Some of these wars were fought against people without divine assistance, especially

---

[22]The Chronicler's account of the defeat of Sennacherib is essentially the same as that of 2 Kings 19:35//Isa. 37:36 and thus not material unique to the Chronicler. The idea of Yahweh fighting alone is important to the Chronicler, but the primary incident of this in the material unique to the Chronicler is found in 2 Chron. 20 (Jehoshaphat's nonsynoptic battle).

[23]*ANET*, 129–35.

[24]Reproduced by George Mendenhall in *The Tenth Generation* (Baltimore: Johns Hopkins Univ. Press, 1973), 46.

wars of aggression by Judah (Azariah, 2 Chron. 22). But in other, more synergistic wars, Yahweh fought for his people while allowing them to participate in the victory (13:16–17).

Closely related to the idea of Yahweh's fighting for his people is the idea of the "fear of the LORD" afflicting the real or potential enemies of Judah. This supernatural element is exemplified in 2 Chronicles 14:14 with the "terror of the LORD" coming upon the cities around Gerar. The Chronicler draws from the old holy-war tradition,[25] in which the "terror of the LORD" came upon the enemy.[26] Normally, this is associated in holy-war ideology with "panic" (*hmm*,[27] *hwm*,[28] or *ḥrd*[29]) in the enemy camp. While the Chronicler does not use any of these terms in 2 Chronicles 14, he does do so in the historical retrospect on the events in 15:6.

The Spoils of War

Regarding the spoils of war, Deuteronomy 2:34–35 records the capture of Sihon:

> At that time we took all his [Sihon, king of Heshbon] towns and completely destroyed them—men, women and children. We left no survivors. But the livestock and the plunder from the towns we had captured we carried off for ourselves.

Cities and people were destroyed; Israel kept only the animals and the inanimate booty of the cities.

Other ancient Near Eastern people practiced the same. For example, Ashurbanipal took booty from his defeated enemies and presented them to his god: "The people and spoil of Elam, which at the command of Assur, Sin, Shamash, Adad . . . I had carried off, the choicest I presented unto my god."[30] The

---

[25]Ex. 15:16; 23:27; Deut. 2:25; 7:20, 23; 11:25; Josh. 2:9, 24; 5:1; 7:5; 10:2; 11:20; 24:12; 1 Sam. 4:7–8; 17:11; 28:5.

[26]1 Chron. 14:17; 2 Chron. 17:10; 19:7; 20:29. Synonyms used by the Chronicler include *yrʾ* (1 Chron. 10:4; 13:12; 22:13; 28:20; 2 Chron. 6:31, 33; 20:3, 15; 32:7, 18, often in the context of "do not fear or be dismayed."

[27]Ex. 14:24; 23:27; Deut. 2:15; Josh. 10:10; Judg. 4:15; 1 Sam. 7:10; 2 Chron. 15:6.
[28]Deut. 7:23.
[29]Judg. 8:12; 1 Sam. 14:15 (3x).
[30]Translation is from Sa-Moon Kang, *Divine War in the Old Testament and in the Ancient Near East* (BZAW 177; Berlin: Walter de Gruyter, 1989), 47.

dedication of the spoils of war to the gods represents one strand of warfare tradition in the ancient Near East.

Another strand of warfare tradition is represented in an inscription from the sixth campaign of Sennacherib:

> From the booty of the lands which (I had conquered), 30,500 bows, 30,500 arrows, I selected from among them, and added to my royal equipment. From the great spoil of enemy-(captives), I apportioned (men) like sheep to all of my camp, to my governors, and to the people of my (large) cities.[31]

Here, Sennacherib retained the booty of his military victory.

In Chronicles, the taking of booty by the victorious Judahite army is described both in Asa's war in 2 Chronicles 14:13–14 and in Jehoshaphat's war in 20:25. Asa and his army appear to have dedicated part of the booty to Yahweh in response to the post-battle prophecy of Azariah: "At that time they sacrificed to the LORD seven hundred head of cattle and seven thousand sheep and goats from the plunder they had brought back" (15:11). After the battle of Asa, in other words, a part of the spoils was sacrificed to Yahweh. Conversely, the plundering of Judah also occurred when Judah met defeat (e.g., at the hands of Shishak in 12:9–11). The spoils of war were expected to belong to the victor. In other words, the Chronicler describes the spoils of victory in a manner wholly consistent with the traditions of the ancient Near East and earlier biblical material.

The Holiness of the Camp

Finally, the Chronicler is highly consistent in his adaptation of ancient warfare themes to his postexilic, theological agenda. He transfers the ancient laws of holiness in the camp to the institution of the temple in Jerusalem. In the older traditions, the army was consecrated to Yahweh (Josh. 3:5). Laws of sexual purity were enforced (1 Sam. 21:5; 2 Sam. 11:11–12), vows were made (Num. 21:2; Judg. 11:36; 1 Sam. 14:24), and the camp had to be kept ritually pure (Deut. 23:9–14). In Chronicles, none of these are included in the warfare narratives. Holiness is still required of the people, but it is a cultic purity transferred from

---

[31]Ibid., 48.

the camp to the nation in its relationship to the temple. The outcome of the battle was decided by the ritual condition not of the camp and its members but of the king and nation as they engaged or failed to engage the divinely mandated cult.

We have traced several elements of ancient warfare from the oldest texts to the later texts of Chronicles. In each case the later work of the Chronicler is thoroughly cognizant of and dependent on the earlier texts. The Chronicler continues the ancient themes of the meaning of defeat, the application of the law of war, holy war as either synergistic and monergistic, the spoils of war, and the holiness of the camp. The idea of holy war, including the practice of *herem*, is still understood as taking place on earth in historical battles.

THE TRAJECTORY: THE ESCHATOLOGY IN CHRONICLES AND BEYOND

Although 1–2 Chronicles continue to develop the theme of warfare, they also advance its concepts in different ways. This two-volume work forms a bridge to what becomes more evident in intertestamental literature and the New Testament, namely, the eschatological. While maintaining a commonality with the past, the Chronicler also finds cosmic significance in the holy-war tradition and introduces a new level of meaning to these accounts. What takes place on earth is, for the Chronicler, directly connected to and reflective of the cosmic and spiritual. It is to this development in and beyond Chronicles that we now turn our attention.

We must first pose an important preliminary question: Does Chronicles have an eschatology? Three basic answers have been given. Some scholars deny that the Chronicler has any eschatological purpose.[32] A mediating position holds that the Chronicler

---

[32]Representing this position is the scholar I believe to be the most influential in Chronicles studies over the last thirty years: the Israeli professor, Sara Japhet. She defines "eschatology in the narrow sense" as what we might commonly call "future eschatology" or anticipation of "the annihilation of the existing world and the birth of a new world of everlasting salvation. It views the eschaton as something beyond history, beyond the time and space of the world as we know it" (see her *The Ideology of the Book of Chronicles and Its Place in Biblical Thought* [BEATAJ 9; Frankfurt: Peter Lang, 1989], 499–500). Contrast this to Japhet's "eschatology in the broader sense," which she defines as "the dawn of the age of salvation . . . in the course of history. According

has a genuinely messianic hope, but a hope based on the preexilic dynastic form rather than an eschatological form.[33] On the other end of the spectrum is a reading of Chronicles that finds the work to be eschatologically oriented in its essence.[34]

A variation of this last category is perhaps the most helpful. In this reading of Chronicles, Saul, David, and Solomon respectively represent judgment, restoration, and final redemption.[35] The successors to Solomon then repeat the cycle of the Saul and David epochs. The Chronicler's age and the intertestamental period that followed were a time of anticipation. God, who once slew Saul and then raised up David, had slain the old Judah at the hand of the Babylonians (the Exile). The future now awaits a new Davidic and Solomonic era.

This eschatological reading of Chronicles is further supported by supernatural elements that come to fuller expression in some intertestamental literature. In the war of Asa (2 Chron. 14), for example, the closing of the war narrative introduces a supernatural element not found in the Abijah narrative (2 Chron.

---

to this definition, eschatology envisions the creation of a new and different world in the context of the existing world, linked to time and history, to space and form" (ibid., 500). Japhet's analysis of the Chronicler's ideology leads her to conclude that "the book of Chronicles cannot be defined as eschatological in any sense of the word. The primary principle underlying the book's world-view is acceptance of the existing world: no change to the world is anticipated in Chronicles" (ibid., 501).

[33]Roland de Vaux, review of W. Rudolph's *Chronikbücher, Esra, und Nehemiah*, *RB* 64 (1957): 278–81.

[34]This is the position of J. Haenel (J. W. Rothstein and J. Haenel, *Das erste Buch Chronik* [KAT 18/2; Leipzig: Reichert, 1927], xliii–xliv) and Gerhard von Rad (*Das Geschichtsbild des chronistischen Werkes* IV/3 [BWANT; Stuttgart: Kohlhammer, 1930], 119–32). W. F. Stinespring ("Eschatology in Chronicles," *JBL* 80 [1961]: 209–19) argued that the Chronicler has an eschatological purpose reflected in the David of history and the David of faith. An example of a Christian eschatological reading of Chronicles is that of A. Noordtzij ("Les Intentions du Chroniste," *RB* 49 [1940]: 161–68), who has argued that the failures of the priesthood and the Davidic house point forward in time to the advent of Christ, the one true shepherd of Israel.

[35]This is the reading of Rudolph Mosis, *Untersuchungen zur Theologie des chronistischen Gesichteswerkes* (FThS 92; Freiburg: Herder, 1973). Mosis argues that Chronicles is not a historical work but a theological system presented as history. He sees the Chronicler's own age as a Davidic epoch, where the temple described in Ezra is preparatory to the ultimate glory of a coming Solomonic era. While there is much to commend in this analysis, I must disagree with it because there is little or nothing in the life of late fifth-century Persian-ruled Judah that can be compared with the era of David.

13). One particular phrase is of interest in this regard: "They were crushed before the LORD and his army[36] [*mḥnh*]" (14:13). There is some question as to whether this applies to a heavenly army or to Asa's troops.[37] Elsewhere in Chronicles, the term *mḥnh* refers to a camp (1 Chron. 9:19) or the temple (2 Chron. 31:2), not to an army. In light of 1 Chronicles 12:22, these are probably Asa's troops:[38] "Day after day men came to help David, until he had a great army, like the army [*mḥnh*] of God."[39]

In the case of Asa's warfare, Yahweh had already won the battle without human participation (2 Chron. 14:12). The "mopping-up" action of the army of Asa, designated in 14:13 as the army of Yahweh, follows the battle proper. Just as the Chronicler had identified the kingdom of Judah in the hands of the sons of David as being, in fact, the kingdom of Yahweh (cf. Abijah's speech, 13:8), so he identifies the army of Judah as the army of Yahweh.

During the intertestamental period, the concept of Yahweh's heavenly army continued to develop beyond the image found in 2 Chronicles 14.[40] The book of 1 Enoch, concerned with angelology and the Day of Judgment, foresees God as coming on Sinai with the mountains shaking and the hills melting like wax. Present with him are his angels: "Behold, he will arrive with ten million of the holy ones in order to execute judgment upon all" (1 En. 1:9).[41] The victory of Yahweh in 1 Enoch resembles that of the Song of the Sea in Exodus 15 in that Yahweh wins the battle without human armies. God fights with his angelic

---

[36]The NIV has "forces."

[37]Simon De Vries, *1 and 2 Chronicles* (FOTL 11; Grand Rapids: Eerdmans, 1989), 299.

[38]See Peter Welten, *Geschichte und Geschictsdarstellung in den Chronikbücher* (WMANT 42; Neukirchener-Vluyn: Neukirchener Verlag, 1973), 134 n.109.

[39]Rudolph (*Chronikbücher,Esra, und Nehemiah* [HAT 1/21; Tbingen: J. C. B. Mohr, 1955], 106) considers this to be the expression of a superlative. Miller (*The Divine Warrior in Early Israel*, 242) understands 1 Chron. 12:22 to be "a comparison between the greatness or size of David's army and the greatness or size of God's army" on the basis of the meeting of Jacob with the angels of God, "This is the army [*mḥnh*; NIV: camp] of God" (Gen. 32:2).

[40]Miller (*The Divine Warrior in Early Israel*, 141–44) traces the development through several post-Hebrew Bible texts.

[41]Translation is from E. Isaac, "1 (Ethiopic Apocalypse of) Enoch," in *The Old Testament Pseudepigrapha*, ed. James H. Charlesworth, 2 vols. (Garden City, N.Y.: Doubleday, 1983), 1:3–89.

army, a phenomenon already seen in the Chronicler's account of the war of Hezekiah when the angel of Yahweh destroyed the enemy (2 Chron. 32:21). Note that in some nonbiblical texts, however, the war of Yahweh is a synergistic battle of Yahweh and his heavenly army with his human army.[42]

The New Testament apocalypses often portray events similar to that in *1 Enoch*. It is with his angels that the Son of Man will return, coming in the clouds and gathering his elect (Mark 8:38; 13:26; cf. 2 Thess. 1:6–10; Rev. 1:7; 19:11–16). This language is certainly dependent on the images of the heavenly army in the Old Testament and in intertestamental literature. At the very least, the New Testament images of the heavenly army are cognizant of the earlier imagery and ultimately of its roots in early holy-war texts.

Whereas Moses, Joshua, and even the judges led Israel into battle in the older narratives, only the legitimate Davidic king does so in Chronicles. The leader of the final, eschatological war is also a Davidic king; in fact, he is the great and final Son of David. The Chronicler looks back at Saul and David and Solomon and sees a paradigm for the present and future—a paradigm he proclaims in order to instill hope among his suffering countrymen. There is much to be learned from the past. In his history, the Chronicler presents the history of the world, and Israel within that world, not only by citing facts and events but also by identifying the narrative of God in the midst of the world's narrative.

The Chronicler foresaw a new David coming (though that would take over four more centuries). In the person of Jesus of

---

[42]See the Qumran text, *The Scroll of the War of the Sons of Light Against the Sons of Darkness*, ed. Yigael Yadin, trans. Batya Rabin and Chaim Rabin (Oxford: Oxford Univ. Press, 1962), 260:

> On the day when the Kittim fall there shall be a mighty encounter and carnage before the God of Israel, for that is a day appointed by Him from of old for a battle of annihilation for the Sons of Darkness, on which there shall engage in a great carnage the congregation of angels and the assembly of men, the Sons of Light and the lot of Darkness, fighting each in communion through the might of God with the sound of a great tumult and the war cry of angels and men for a day of doom. (1QM 1:9–11)

This is a clear intertestamental example of divinely sanctioned ḥerem. The destruction of the enemies by Yahweh and his people here is complete.

Nazareth, the new and final David did come to Israel. Everything was present in him, just as all things were present in the first David. And yet it was hidden within his assumed humanity. All the future of the eschatological kingdom was there—no evil, no pain, no illness, not even death itself could stand in his presence. Yet the new David, like the first, could be and was in fact subjected to vicious attack. David of old fought war after war and yet always emerged victorious. The new David too was attacked—in fact, crucified. Yet like the David of old, the new David could not be defeated. Easter morning brought final victory to the house of David, the house of Judah, the house of Israel—and the house of Adam.

It is within that Davidic epoch that the church lives out its existence. He is declared to be king by his followers despite what his enemies might say of him. The church follows by faith, living in time and space the eschatological reality of the final Son of David:

> I charge you to keep this command without spot or blame until the appearing of our Lord Jesus Christ, which God will bring about in his own time—God, the blessed and only Ruler, the King of kings and Lord of lords, who alone is immortal and who lives in unapproachable light, whom no one has seen or can see. To him be honor and might forever. Amen. (1 Tim. 6:13–16)

> Therefore God exalted him to the highest place
> and gave him the name that is above every name,
> that at the name of Jesus every knee should bow,
> in heaven and on earth and under the earth,
> and every tongue confess that Jesus Christ is Lord,
> to the glory of God the Father. (Phil. 2:9–11)

This is the defining reality for the Christian, one that is shared by the supporters of the "first David" as they saw him at Ziklag and, later, by the Chronicler as he looked beyond the humiliation of Persian rule toward a future brightened by the second David.

This present Davidic age is to be succeeded in history by a new Solomonic era. This is the future of the universe, the age of the new temple, fully present in the incarnate Christ and victoriously displayed in the eschaton. The shift from the present

Davidic epoch to a future Solomonic epoch is the shift from a lived theology of the cross to a manifested theology of glory. This signals the great and final coronation feast. The feasts that were shared by those who celebrated David's coronation at Hebron (1 Chron. 12:38–40) and Solomon's in Jerusalem (29:20–22), for all their joy, are insignificant when compared to the feast that awaits all believers. That eschatological feast brings together all the scattered children of God—not only those of Israel but those separated children of Adam as well (cf. 1 Chron. 1:1). That anticipated eternal feast even now sustains the church on earth.

Both the Chronicler and the intertestamental literature utilize the ancient law of *herem*. In the unique warfare narrative of 2 Chronicles 20, Jehoshaphat faced a "vast army" (20:2) whose size alarmed Jehoshaphat despite his own army of 1,160,000 troops (17:14–18). But before the battle began, "the LORD set ambushes," and the coalition of Ammon, Moab, and Mount Seir rose up against each other and annihilated each other (20:22–23).[43] All that was left was for the Judahites to gather the booty in keeping with the law of Deuteronomy 20:13–14. Significantly, it was not the army of Jehoshaphat but God himself who destroyed the enemy.

The imposition of the *herem* ban itself is identifiable in the New Testament's eschatological texts. Note, for example, the familiar text from 2 Peter 3:7, 10, 13:

> By the same word the present heavens and earth are reserved for fire, being kept for the day of judgment and destruction of ungodly men....
>
> But the day of the Lord will come like a thief. The heavens will disappear with a roar; the elements will be destroyed by fire, and the earth and everything in it will be laid bare....
>
> But in keeping with his promise we are looking forward to a new heaven and a new earth, the home of righteousness.

---

[43]Enemy armies self-destruct in other biblical texts as well. See, e.g., Judg. 7:22; Ezek. 38:21; Hag. 2:22; Zech. 14:13. It is also of interest that the text of 2 Kings 3, which some scholars feels is replaced by 2 Chron. 20, also has the enemy killing each other (2 Kings 3:22–23). Nonbiblical ancient Near Eastern accounts also describe the self-destruction of armies (Moshe Weinfeld, "Divine Intervention in War in Ancient Israel and in the Ancient Near East," in *History, Historiography and Interpretation*, ed. H. Tadmor and M. Weinfeld [Jerusalem: Magnes, 1983], 121–47).

Although neither 2 Peter nor any other New Testament text speaks specifically of the *herem* of the Old Testament, the image of the total destruction of the entire earth is a prevalent theme in the eschatology of the New Testament.

The preaching of Jesus himself often pointed toward a kingdom of God that would involve a violent and radical alteration of all creation. In the parable of the weeds, Matthew records these words:

> As the weeds are pulled up and burned in the fire, so it will be at the end of the age. The Son of Man will send out his angels, and they will weed out of his kingdom everything that causes sin and all who do evil. They will throw them into the fiery furnace, where there will be weeping and gnashing of teeth. Then the righteous will shine like the sun in the kingdom of their Father. He who has ears, let him hear. (Matt. 13:40–43)

Jesus further spoke of a separation of the sheep from the goats when the Son of Man comes in his glory. To the goats on his left, he speaks words of ultimate destruction: "Depart from me, you who are cursed, into the eternal fire prepared for the devil and his angels" (Matt. 25:41).

How, then, does the New Testament pick up on these images of God as warrior? The center of the New Testament is the story of Jesus. The reader is introduced to him in the infancy narratives—what could be further from the story of a warrior God? He is seen preaching and teaching, healing, feeding the multitudes, and even dying at the hands of humanity. And yet permeating the New Testament is an entirely different vision of Jesus. In the eschatology of the New Testament, he is seen not as a meek and gentle Savior but as the conquering King.

CONTINUITY BETWEEN THE TESTAMENTS: THE ESCHATOLOGICAL CONNECTION

How, then, does the trajectory I have developed help us to understand the *herem* ban and the continuity of the Testaments? Let me summarize by suggesting that the connection between the earliest holy-war texts with their law of *herem* and the New Testament is an eschatological connection. The God who commanded and, at times, personally executed *herem* against the enemies of Israel is the same God who will execute judgment and destruction at the end of time.

The picture of Jesus as conqueror is not unexpected, given the development of the biblical images of warfare and the destruction of all who oppose the God of Israel. When Israel entered Canaan, other nations occupied the land. They stood in opposition not only to the nation but also to the God who had given the land to Israel. The imposition of the ban or *herem* on these nations was a real and bloody series of events, acted out in space and time. In this regard, Israel exercised the same violent tactics in victory as other nations.

In time, the genocidal destruction of the opposing nations took on new and more cosmic proportions. By the end of the Old Testament period, the Chronicler made tremendous theological use of the old holy-war tradition. Battles involving huge numbers of troops are settled by divine action on the battlefield. The supernatural permeates this theological history. God acts in time and history with and for Israel. Even his angels fight for his people. To oppose the people of God is to oppose God himself and inevitably results in the utter destruction of his enemies.

The apocalyptic literature of the intertestamental period elevates this warfare and *herem* to even greater proportions. Divinely executed genocide is no longer exercised in real time but at the end of time, ushering in a new and glorious era for the people of God. Yahweh, his angels, and his people are the victors; the enemies of God are the vanquished.

The powerful images of intertestamental eschatology form a matrix in which the ministry of Jesus of Nazareth and the ministry of the apostles took place. According to the New Testament, Jesus the judge will destroy the earth and its rebellious inhabitants and, in so doing, inaugurate his glorious kingdom. Like the ancient holy-war imposition of *herem*, the eschatological imposition is one of justice and righteousness. Like the later texts, it occurs with cosmic force at the end of time and ushers in a new era.

Such images are not to be understood as paradigms for implementation by any modern nation, however. Uniquely, ancient Israel was at once both "church" and "state." That is to say, they had a theological identity as a kingdom of priests and a holy nation as well as that of a political entity. The refrain "I will take you as my own people, and I will be your God" (Ex. 6:7; cf. Lev. 26:12; Ps. 95:7; Jer. 11:4) reflects a complex but essential relationship between the Lord and his people.

Israel was a chosen people, called from the nations of the world to bear a unique and special relationship to God. Deuteronomy provides a clear explication of that identity granted in the calling of the patriarch Abraham in Genesis 12: "For you are a people holy to the LORD your God. The LORD your God has chosen you out of all the peoples on the face of the earth to be his people, his treasured possession" (Deut. 7:6). From this flowed the salvific work of God in redeeming Israel from Egyptian bondage:

> You yourselves have seen what I did to Egypt, and how I carried you on eagles' wings and brought you to myself. Now if you obey me fully and keep my covenant, then out of all nations you will be my treasured possession. Although the whole earth is mine, you will be for me a kingdom of priests and a holy nation. (Ex. 19:4–6a)

This people, though not numerous or powerful, nevertheless bore a unique identity with the Lord who rules all the earth.

Israel had no other identity in the world other than that of the people of God. This was not external to their identity; it constituted their identity. Of no other people does God say, "Be holy because I, the LORD your God, am holy" (Lev. 19:2). The Lord was always "your God," and Israel was always "his people." The prophet Isaiah, in comforting his people, reminds them that they are the servants of Yahweh, chosen in Jacob, descendants of Abraham (Isa. 41:8).

Israel, along with its theological identity, also had a political identity. King Abijah, facing the rebellious northern tribes of Israel in battle, identified the very throne of Judah as "the kingdom of the LORD, which is in the hands of David's descendants" (2 Chron. 13:8). Even before the establishment of the Davidic kingship, Israel was a nation with its own political identity, whether in Egypt or in the Promised Land. It is for this reason that the ancient law of war was given before they entered the land that would be their home. Israel would interact with the nations of the world not only in trade but in warfare as well. It would be in constant danger from surrounding peoples, especially the people of the land: the Hittites, the Amorites, the Canaanites, the Perizzites, the Hivites, and the Jebusites. These nations were to be utterly destroyed (Deut. 20:16–18), for by doing so the life of the nation in the land would be assured. Israel was not to fear because Yahweh their God would fight for them. To attempt to withstand Israel was to attempt to withstand Yahweh himself.

Such is not the case of the New Testament church, however. She has no identity except as the people of God. The church has no territorial or political boundaries. She does not raise armies or fight battles with weapons ancient or modern. Violence between nations still does occur, of course, and individual members of the church are found in the governments and militaries of many earthly nations. But as to the church herself, her identity is only as a theological entity, whose warfare is spiritual, not fleshly.

Until the eschaton, the church will suffer in this world, especially at the hands of God's enemies. Yet those who attack the church attack her Lord and, in the end, will meet the same fate as the ancient enemies of Israel. The great and final *herem* will be imposed not by the church but by the Lord of the church. Thus, vengeance belongs to the Lord.

How does this, then, speak to the ethics of modern warfare and the recurring problem of genocide? No political, geography-bound nation on earth today can claim to be the people of God as ancient Israel once claimed. That distinction of "people of God" belongs only to the church, and the church does not bear arms. No human can impose *herem* on other humans. When Israel imposed the ban, they did so by divine command. In such cases, Israel acted in synergy with their God. In later literature, it is God himself who not only imposed but executed *herem*. In the same way God will impose it again at the end of time not against a particular nation but against all who stand opposed to him and his kingdom.

Only the Lord who gives life can take life. This is not to argue a pacifist position, since God can and does grant to human rulers the sword of justice. But he does not grant a sword of aggression even to kings and princes. With St. Augustine, a long tradition of the Western church has maintained that a Christian can participate in war, but only if it is a just war.

To engage in genocide (apart from divine command of *herem* given to Israel) is simply to commit mass murder. For this reason, modern nations have sought to outlaw such actions. For example, the Geneva Convention attempts to protect the life of noncombatants and civilian populations even in times of intense combat. In an age of nuclear, biological, and chemical warfare (the so-called "weapons of mass destruction") and devastating "conventional" weapons, such protections have little practical value. In the face of all this, such conventions seem futile. As desperately as some seek to prevent genocide, just as desperately others seek to impose it on their enemies.

These resolutions continue to fail to accomplish their good and lofty goals ultimately not for political and military reasons, but for theological reasons. The world is still in rebellion against God, assuming for itself the prerogatives that belong only to him. Declaring a nation or a people to be worthy of extinction is the right of the Creator alone, not of the creature. To do so is to blaspheme the Divine by the deification of the human. Even if one nation declares itself to be so morally righteous that it may sit in judgment on another nation, in the end God will himself judge that nation in his perfect justice.

At the beginning of this essay I asked: How could a God of love, known in the pages of the New Testament as the meek and gentle Lamb of God, command such brutal practices? Should a wedge be placed between the Old and New Testaments in order to preserve the integrity of both? Can there be a connection between these ancient accounts of God's people Israel and the image of God as Savior so prevalent in the Gospels?

A first answer to these questions has to do with the very character of God. He is holy, demanding the response of Isaiah: "'Woe to me!' I cried. 'I am ruined! For I am a man of unclean lips, and I live among a people of unclean lips, and my eyes have seen the King, the LORD Almighty'" (Isa. 6:5). God is not merely a reflection of human culture or what the imaginations of the human heart may conjecture he should be like. His holiness is far beyond that of human comprehension, involving not only his ethical purity but also his supreme majesty and absolute transcendence. Before him nothing sinful may stand.

Not only is God holy; he is also just. His justice cannot be analogized by any human system of justice. Moses declared, "He is the Rock, his works are perfect, and all his ways are just. A faithful God who does no wrong, upright and just is he"

(Deut. 32:4). If there is a problem in understanding God's commands and actions, the problem resides not in him but in human limitations. His justice is pure and righteous, even when it imposes the destruction of his enemies either in time and history or beyond time and history, that is to say, eschatologically.

A more pertinent question than why God commanded such brutal practices as the extermination of the Canaanites is why he did not command the destruction of the entire human race in time and history. He once did so at the time of Noah, but even then he preserved a remnant in the ark. He used human armies against his own people in "reverse holy war" but always preserved a remnant. The question is truly not one about God's love but about his justice, once acted out in history as it will be on the last day. He preserved then and will always preserve his people.

The ultimate answer to those questions, however, is found only in the person of Jesus Christ, whom we see in the New Testament to be both Lamb and Judge. The command of God to exterminate an enemy reflects his holiness and justice, but that holiness and justice cannot be understood apart from the same God's mercy, grace, and long-suffering. Central to the teaching of the New Testament is that collision of holiness and justice with mercy and grace found in the holy, innocent suffering and death of Jesus. In his death he bore the full wrath of God's justice in the place of the entire human race. Here is the Lamb, the sacrifice for all who are at enmity with God. The world stands condemned under God's perfect holiness and justice. It was into that mass of condemned humanity that God sent his Son to bring rescue, life, and salvation to all who believe. Thus, the justice of God is transformed by his mercy.

In the eschatological Jesus is found the unity of time and eternity and the unity of both Testaments. It is he who once said, "You diligently study the Scriptures because you think that by them you possess eternal life. These are the Scriptures that testify about me" (John 5:39). He who is the Lamb will be seen again as Judge. All nations will stand before him and receive his righteous judgment. His remnant is preserved for eternity. His enemies are destroyed in his great and final and just *herem*.

In history, as ancient Israel fought her wars, the ultimate victory of God was lived out. It is to that victory that God invites the world through the Lamb. At the end of time the eschatological judgment of *herem* will be spoken. Until then, God's people will continue to be drawn from every nation, every people, and every tongue. They will not fear, for Yahweh, their God, will fight for them.

RESPONSES TO
DANIEL L. GARD

A RESPONSE TO DANIEL L. GARD

C. S. Cowles

Daniel Gard has stitched together texts of genocidal *ḥerem* to form a "trajectory" of "eschatological continuity ... between the Old and New Testaments" that is ingenious. Though faithful to his "a priori creedal assertion" regarding the reliability of the Scripture "as a historical text,"[1] his imaginatively crafted project raises critical issues that must be addressed.

Genocide in the ancient world. Gard notes that when it comes to genocide, "the nation of Israel was not unique ... in the ancient Near East. They were following the practices of other nations, which practiced their own equivalent of *ḥerem*." The examples he cites, however, occurred three to four centuries *after* the Conquest. Thus, it was not Israel who followed "the practices of other nations," but the nations who adopted Israel's ideology and practice. What is amazing, given the prevalence of genocide in the twentieth century, is that so few nations followed Israel's lead. Idolatrous nations showed more compassion toward defeated enemies than the Israelites did.

Canaanite genocide and God's justice. A sense of unreality inevitably attends our reading of anything from which we are separated so far in time. This is especially evident in Gard's essay, where he clinically dissects Old Testament genocidal atrocities with the dispassionate detachment of a pest-control operator discussing the extermination of termites. There is a noticeable absence of any sense that real people are being slaughtered—

---

[1] See also Daniel G. Reid and Tremper Longman III, "When God Declares War," *Christianity Today* (Oct. 28, 1996), 17.

human beings created in the image of God and for whom Jesus died. He betrays not the slightest sympathy for the nations who are "utterly destroyed so that nothing that breathed should live."

The reason Gard can speak of Canaanite genocide with such indifference is his belief that the "imposition of *herem* ... is one of justice and righteousness." This conclusion is derived from the theological conviction that "not only is God holy; he is also just." Yet, realizing how impossible it is to sustain any notion of justice in the face of genocide, ancient or modern, Gard offers the caveat that "[God's] justice cannot be analogized by any human system of justice."

Such a disingenuous way of "dodging the bullet" cannot be sustained. If we believe, as Gard does, that "revelation takes place not only through the written Scripture but also through the acts of God in history" and that "even in the brutality of ancient warfare, God reveals himself," then we have an abundance of objective evidence in the Old Testament by which to assess God's supposed justice. Achan, for instance, may have been justly condemned for violating "the ban" placed on Jericho's plunder, but where is the justice in stoning and burning "his sons and daughters" with him (Josh. 7:24–25)? What makes this judgment even more outrageous is that what was forbidden at Jericho was permitted at Ai.

We see this same kind of arbitrariness in Moses' manual of war in Deuteronomy 20, where only the men were to be killed when the Israelites conquered distant cities (Deut. 20:10–15). When it came to nearby cities, however, the command was to "not leave alive anything that breathes.... Completely destroy them" (20:16–17). The reason the latter were to be annihilated and the former spared had nothing to do with their relative degree of idolatry or moral corruption, but everything to do with geographical proximity.

Likewise, the Gibeonites were spared, not because they were more righteous than other Canaanites but because Joshua would not break his word even though he had been deceived. In the Gibeonite affair, Joshua disobeyed the clear command of Moses to "destroy" the Canaanites "totally" and "show them no mercy" (Deut. 7:2). Unlike Achan, however, neither he nor his family were stoned and burned. What kind of justice was that?

The annihilation of the Amalekites in Samuel's day had nothing to do with justice and everything to do with vengeance.

The hapless descendents of Amalek were mercilessly and unjustly slaughtered for something their ancestors had done more than two centuries earlier. What makes this even more inexplicable is that this supposedly divine directive violated God's earlier commandment to Moses that "fathers shall not be put to death for their children, nor children put to death for their fathers; each is to die for his own sin" (Deut. 24:16). We have the odd circumstance of God's commands violating God's laws.

When the eleven tribes "inquired of the LORD" (Judg. 20:27) whether they should go to war against the Benjamites to avenge the rape and killing of an Ephraimite's concubine (19:12–30), "the LORD responded, 'Go, for tomorrow I will give them into your hands'" (20:28). After defeating their army, the men of Israel attacked their defenseless towns and put all the women and children "to the sword" (20:48).

The genocidal slaughter was not over, however. In order to provide wives for the six hundred Benjamite warriors who had fled to the hills and thus to repopulate that tribe, the Israelites turned on the inhabitants of one of their own cities who had refused to join in the genocidal war against fellow tribesmen. Soldiers were instructed to go and kill all the men, women, and children of Jabesh Gilead except for "young women who had never slept with a man" (Judg. 21:12). These virgins were then forcefully "seized" by the surviving Benjamite warriors as wives (21:10–24). In all of this internecine slaughter of Israelite women and children and the forcible rape of young virgins, where was God's justice being displayed? There is one redeeming feature of this otherwise sordid saga of Israel's genocidal fury turned against itself: Ḥerem as an ideology and a strategy of Yahweh war was utterly discredited and renounced. Never again would the Israelites resort to genocide in any of their wars.

Most indefensible, in terms of justice, was the intentional slaughter of children, both Canaanite and Israelite. "Listen," protests Ivan in Dostoyevsky's *The Brothers Karamazov*, "even if we assume that every person must suffer because his suffering is necessary to pay for eternal harmony, still do tell me, for God's sake, where the children come in?"[2] Good question. Why were children especially targeted? What evil had they done? Can we just dismiss them, like Timothy McVeigh in the Oklahoma City

---

[2]Fyodor Dostoyevsky, *The Brothers Karamazov* (New York: Bantam, 1970), 294.

bombing, as so much "collateral damage?" To justify the killing of "little children," whom Jesus blessed and declared to be "the greatest in the kingdom of heaven" (Matt. 18:3–4), by appealing to a doctrine of total depravity,[3] not only undercuts the doctrines of creation, redemption, and grace but levels a direct assault on John's categorical claim that "God is love" (1 John 4:8, 16). Genocide at any time, in any place, for any reason, mocks, defames, and destroys any notion of justice. It is, in a word, anti-Christ.

Eschatology. Gard's basic thesis is that there is a "trajectory" of divinely initiated and sanctioned genocide that begins with the annihilation of the Canaanites in "real time" and concludes with the genocidal destruction of the "ungodly" at "the end of time." It is hard to imagine, however, anything more discontinuous, more unrelated, and more antithetical than the wanton extermination of the Canaanites without the slightest regard for the relative guilt or innocence of individuals on the one hand, and the final judgment presided over by "the Lamb that was slain from the creation of the world" (Rev. 13:8) on the other. When the nations stand before the "great white throne" (20:11), no fetuses will be ripped out of mother's wombs, no babies will be consigned to hell, and no children will be banished into "outer darkness." No one will be "thrown into the lake of fire" (20:15) because of their race, nationality, or religious affiliation. No one will hear, "Depart from me" (Matt. 7:23 KJV), just because of the accident of having been born in the wrong place at the wrong time. Nor will any one suffer the eternal torments of being eternally separated from God because of the sins of their ancestors.

Canaanite genocide was executed by fallible and sinful Israelites just as prone to idolatry, disobedience, and wickedness as the people they destroyed. The final judgment will be presided over by a God who "was reconciling the world to himself in Christ" (2 Cor. 5:19); a God who "demonstrates His own love toward us, in that while we were yet sinners, Christ died

---

[3]Gard implies this when, in justifying "the extermination of the Canaanites," he asks "why [God] did not command the destruction of the entire human race in time and history." Tremper Longman III, in his essay states, "The Bible does not understand the destruction of the . . . children of these cities as a slaughter of innocents. Not even the children are considered innocent. They are all part of an inherently wicked culture."

for us" (Rom. 5:8 NASB); a God "who wants all men to be saved and to come to a knowledge of the truth" (1 Tim. 2:4); a God in Christ who treated Canaanites and foreigners with as much compassion, dignity, and respect as any Israelite; a God who "is kind to the ungrateful and wicked"—and "merciful" (Luke 6:35–36); a God whose righteous judgments at the end of time will be entirely consistent with his self-disclosure in the person of his incarnate Son Jesus; a God in Christ who would rather be crucified than crucify, who would rather be destroyed than destroy, who would rather die than damn, and who did!

There is a heaven to gain and a hell to shun. Those who finally spend eternity separated from their loving Creator-Redeemer will do so only by intentionally stepping over the dead body of the crucified Christ and by turning their backs on the gracious invitation of the risen Lord: "Come to me, all you who are weary and burdened, and I will give you rest" (Matt. 11:28). As they go, a tear will course down our Savior's cheek.

A RESPONSE TO DANIEL L. GARD

Eugene H. Merrill

I begin my interaction with Professor Gard's contribution to a discussion on Old Testament genocide by commending him for presenting his case with conviction and clarity. His focus on eschatology as a unifying principle has enabled him to make his argument in an unusually cohesive manner. Having said that, however, there appears to be a "straitjacketing" imposition of a *heilsgeschichtliche* scheme that forces certain elements of his argument to founder, or at least to lack persuasiveness. Before that and other issues are addressed, it may be helpful to outline Gard's approach as follows: (1) his presuppositions concerning Scripture, eschatology, and the future role of Israel; (2) his understanding of the nature of God; (3) his understanding of the nature of holy war; and (4) his understanding of the nature of sacred history. As his own paper makes clear, these elements are inextricably linked and mutually informing.

Basic presuppositions. After addressing the tension that inevitably arises in contrasting the Old Testament warrior God with the New Testament Lamb of God, the gentle Jesus, Gard makes clear that no Marcionite wedge can be driven between the Old and New Testaments, nor can one dispense with the Old Testament accounts of warfare and genocide by "rejecting them out of hand as having any valid history." In fact, he insists that not just the records of the events but the very events themselves are revelatory—"even in the brutality of ancient warfare, God reveals himself." But such texts must be read in their canonical contexts with a view toward their possible typological significance. The hermeneutics undergirding this aspect of Gard's view of Scripture will be addressed presently. Suffice it to say for now that any deficiency in his argument cannot be attributed to a deficient understanding of the nature of the Bible.

By eschatology Gard refers primarily to New Testament and end-times events, primarily the latter. His insistence that holy-war episodes in the Old Testament were genuinely historical events leads him to state categorically that eschatological warfare must also be understood in literal terms since the Old Testament examples are typical of that which is to come. In fact, the "connection between the earliest holy-war texts with their law of herem and the New Testament is an eschatological connection." To Gard, the only factor that can, in the final analysis, lead to a proper understanding of Old Testament genocide is its persistent future orientation. Old Testament instances of holy war serve to warn of God's great day of judgment to come.

Given his eschatological tradition, one is not surprised at Gard's omission of any reference to the role of Israel in eschatological times. He clearly sees no such role since, in his view, the church has become the exclusive people of God, a people who obviously have incorporated the Jew (or Israel) as well. Of course, he is not to be faulted for this omission in terms of holy-war theology, for no system makes allowance for Israel's prosecution of holy war in the future except perhaps as Israel herself is delivered by the Lord in the Tribulation and Millennium, and that only in dispensational hermeneutics.

The nature of God. A major conundrum for those who struggle with the moral and ethical issues of holy war is the apparent contradiction between its sanction—indeed, its mandate—in the Old Testament and its lack of attention in the teachings of Jesus and the apostles in the New Testament, with the already-noted exception of eschatological texts. Put bluntly, one can legitimately ask: Is the God of the Old Testament also the God of the New Testament?

Curiously, Gard does not address this question head-on, though there can be no doubt as to his answer in the final analysis. The "warrior" God of the Old Testament is the God and Father of our Lord Jesus Christ. This is seen primarily both in the eschatological themes that bind the Testaments together and in the very character of God, the everlasting One.

As for the eschatological connection, Gard makes three observations. (1) The Chronicler, at the end of the Old Testament period, makes great use of ancient holy-war traditions, thus suggesting that holy war was not limited to the distant past. (2) The apocalyptic literature of the Second Temple period "elevates this warfare and *herem* to even greater proportions." Far from being passé, Judaism understood that the work of the warrior God was yet unfinished and had to reach finality in an age to come. (3) The New Testament teaches that Jesus will come as judge to destroy the earth and its rebellious inhabitants and in so doing will inaugurate his glorious kingdom. This unbroken skein of eschatological hope can lead to no other conclusion than that the God of Israel is the God of the church and that his role as warrior permeates both dispensations.

As to the character of God providing a linkage between his warrior image in the Old Testament and that of Savior in the Gospels, Gard focuses on two attributes of God that are transtestamental and one query that demands an answer. He correctly asserts that God is intrinsically holy and "not merely a reflection of human culture or what the imaginations of the human heart may conjecture he should be like." A corollary to this is that "before him nothing sinful may stand." Since this is a matter of the *nature* of God and not merely a functional aspect, one can expect that sin in every generation must be dealt with in the same way, namely, by radical and total extermination. Concomitant with his holiness is God's justice, which, as Gard helpfully suggests, may not always be understandable and palatable to the human mind but which cannot, for that reason alone, be rejected as unworthy of him. "If there is a problem in understanding God's commands and actions," Gard observes, "the problem resides not in him but in human limitations."

The question Gard asks is most pertinent and provocative: If God destroyed the Canaanites by genocide, why has he not by now destroyed the entire human race? The answer is that he did already, at least for the most part, in the universal deluge. And in line with his eschatological theme, Gard reminds us that a Canaanite "genocide" yet remains in the future and final day of God's judgment.

The nature of holy war. A less-convincing part of Professor Gard's presentation is his portrayal of Old Testament holy war in both definitional and applicational terms. Part of the problem, of course, is the lack of any scholarly consensus as to the sine qua non of such conflict to begin with. Following von Rad's thirteen characteristics, most of the battle accounts of the Old Testament can be loosely labeled "holy war." Gard, sensing the problems inherent in such breadth of definition, speaks of holy war in its purest form as consisting of the devotion of all spoils to Yahweh and the destruction of all life. Less "pure" forms allowed certain exemptions such as women, children, and livestock, but men invariably must be slain, particularly those of the seven Canaanite nations. Having said all that, however, he goes on to speak of postexilic *ḥerem* as demanding no death at all, in one instance at least (Ezra 10:8). On the other hand, the examples of its practice that he cites from the Chronicler are irrelevant to the postexilic period because without exception they refer to preexilic events.

Further evidence of Gard's fuzziness in terms of definition and limitation of holy war is his lumping together of all of Deuteronomy 20 as an exposition of holy-war ideology and practice. Only in the broadest sense can verses 1–15 qualify as such, for although certain features (such as Yahweh's participation [vv. 1, 4] and the presence of the priests [vv. 2–3]) are also elements of holy war, Gard's own criteria of "pure" holy war—that is, the devotion of spoils of war to Yahweh and the destruction of all life—are missing.

True (or "pure") holy war is described in verses 16–20, a section commencing with a strong adversative construction—"but" or "on the other hand." Here the targets are the Canaanite nations and the result is *ḥerem*, the total annihilation of all living things.

Other proposed examples, such as Ahaziah's defeat at the hands of Jehu (2 Chron. 22:7) and the exile of the southern kingdom as a whole (36:17), fail to conform to holy-war criteria even though Yahweh was participatory. Gard himself is forced to concede that Israel was never "subject to the complete annihilation of genocide." Nor did Yahweh ever impose *ḥerem* against Israel "in its fullest sense." In light of these caveats, it is unlikely that these examples and certain others adduced in his paper can properly fall within the category of holy war.

The nature of history. The most troubling feature of Gard's approach is his view of biblical history, one that proceeds on typical and analogical grounds to periodize history through a patternism that has little or no support except as an a priori conceptual construct. He begins by suggesting that events of the Old Testament may serve as types of what is to come in the New Testament—an understanding of the Bible with which many scholars would agree. The problem lies with his arbitrary assertion that Saul, David, and Solomon represent the historical periods of judgment, restoration, and final redemption, respectively. How the dismal failure of Solomon and his monarchy can be understood as final redemption is not at all clear.

But Gard goes on to argue that the cycle begins again after Solomon with new "Saul" and "David" epochs. The former is brought to an end with the Babylonian exile, which (to Gard) is a second slaying of Saul. There remained, then, a new Davidic and Solomonic era. This new era will feature restoration under David *redivivus*, the Son of David, who will lead the final eschatological battle. This will usher in the Solomonic final redemption.

This entire scenario Gard claims to find in the writings of the Chronicler, though he offers little evidence. According to this epochal pattern, the church now lives in the Davidic age, one to be followed by the Solomonic, which is "the future of the universe, the age of the new temple, fully present in ... the eschaton." As suggested already, the ruinous collapse of the united monarchy because of Solomon's moral and spiritual perfidy hardly serves well as a paradigm against which to view eschatological glory and victory.

Conclusion. Professor Gard has provided an important and heuristic insight into the issue of genocide continuity/discontinuity with his emphasis on eschatology as a binding thematic and structural device. Putting aside for the moment some rather strong reservations about his definition of holy war and his historical patternism, Gard's contribution is much appreciated as a hermeneutical and theological step forward.

A RESPONSE TO DANIEL L. GARD

Tremper Longman III

On many points, my own view is closer to Gard's than either to Merrill's or (especially) to Cowles's positions. I too recognize and describe the eschatological continuity between the Testaments (see my phase 5). For this reason, my response to Gard will be short. However, I do find deficiencies in his description of the biblical concept of Old Testament and New Testament holy war and would like to briefly point these out. As I delineate what I take to be inadequacies in his presentation, I will not fully explicate my alternative approach but simply refer the reader to my own chapter.

I will begin by admitting that I found Gard's arguments confusing on several accounts. For instance, I would challenge the idea that the "simplest way to develop the trajectory from the earliest warfare narratives through to the end of the Old Testament, through the intertestamental period, and on into the New Testament is to trace particular themes in which there is a large degree of consistency." In the first place, I was not always sure of the significance of a point that he was trying to make from this chosen themes. The first theme is the theme of defeat. He rightly points out that the Old Testament narrates the defeat of Israel and reflects on its meaning. This is true of early and late texts. But then he suggests that "there are also important differences in Chronicles." He describes Chronicles as presenting a narrative of defeat taking place during the generation that offended Yahweh (immediate retribution), where human armies did not determine the defeat and where defeat was linked to the faithlessness of king and people. But how is this different from the defeat of Ai in Joshua 7 or the defeat of the Israelites under Hophni and Phinehas in 1 Samuel 4? And if there is no difference, how is there a trajectory from early holy-war accounts to later ones?

Take as a second example his comments on monergism and synergism—that is, whether God is pictured fighting alone on behalf of Israel or together with Israel. In his description at this point of his paper, he writes that in some battles the emphasis is on God's fighting *for* his people and in others *with* his people. He cites as examples of the first the crossing of the Re(e)d Sea and descriptions of some battles in Chronicles, which he takes as early accounts and late accounts. Indeed in this section he concludes that "the two motifs of Yahweh fighting alone and Yahweh fighting in conjunction with the people are interwoven in the biblical warfare narratives." True enough, but it leaves the reader wondering how this provides the basis of a trajectory.

In a latter section entitled "Continuity Between the Testaments: The Eschatological Connection," Gard implies that there was a development from the early wars to the more cosmic descriptions of battles in Chronicles, where "the genocidal destruction of the opposing nations took on new and more cosmic proportions." My problem with this is not only the confusing nature of the discussion but also the idea that there is an evolution from a noncosmic to a cosmic understanding of holy war. After all, not only was the defeat of Egypt at the Re(e)d Sea accomplished through almost exclusively divine action (though Moses had to pray and hold up the rod that symbolized God's presence), but the defeat of Egypt from beginning to end was understood as successful war waged against the Egyptian gods (Ex. 12:12; Num. 33:4). I am not sure how much more cosmic this very early holy-war account could be.

Thus, I question the kind of chronological development that Gard suggests that provides the foundation for his trajectory. In any case, it strikes me as odd that he would appeal to Chronicles as the late bridge from the Old Testament to the New Testament via the intertestamental literature. Much more relevant, as I tried to point out in my chapter, and functioning the same way as he uses the book of Chronicles, is the apocalyptic literature of the Old Testament—texts such as Daniel 7 and Zechariah

14. Gard acknowledges a role of this literature in a short paragraph of three sentences as he moves from Chronicles to the intertestamental literature, but this is surely not adequate, since it is books such as Zechariah and especially Daniel that are explicitly appropriated in the apocalyptic passages of the New Testament (e.g., Mark 13 and parallels, the book of Revelation).

Further, Gard's analysis of New Testament holy war also bypasses what I call phase 4 and presses on immediately to phase 5. This is a problem because the passages I cite from the Gospels and the New Testament letters both indicate that the New Testament writers themselves understood the spiritual warfare of the present age as a continuation of the physical warfare of the Old Testament and as an anticipation of the final battle of the end times.

In summary, I find myself in agreement with Gard's main conclusion but in the awkward position of disagreeing with how he arrives at his conclusion. With all due respect, I offer as a fully and more straightforward account the description in my chapter.

Chapter Four

THE CASE FOR SPIRITUAL CONTINUITY

Tremper Longman III

THE CASE FOR
SPIRITUAL CONTINUITY

Tremper Longman III

Modern Americans have a difficult time understanding the mindset of an Islamic *mujahaddin* (holy warrior) like Osama bin Laden. His ideas and rhetoric seem so foreign from those of a modern Western democracy that prides itself on its cultural tolerance. However, Christians who know their Bible should understand exactly what motivates his beliefs and actions. Two Old Testament ideas are analogous to the ideology that fuels bin Laden's passionate ideology: sacred space and *herem* warfare.

Bin Laden's anger toward the West is triggered at least in part by the presence of Westerners in Saudi Arabia. To most Muslims the sacred precincts are limited to areas connected to the holy places at Mecca and Medina. Bin Laden has expanded this idea of sacred space to include the entirety of the peninsula and thus wants all infidels expelled from Saudi Arabia. The analogy with the Old Testament may be found in the sacred precincts surrounding the tabernacle/temple in the Old Testament.[1] The sanctuary was surrounded by circles of holiness that permitted only certain types of people to be admitted into God's presence. This sentiment continued as long as the Second Temple remained in existence; note how riots were set off when some suspected Paul had brought a Gentile into the court of the temple (Acts 21:27–29).

---

[1]See T. Longman III, *Immanuel in Our Place: Seeing Christ in Israel's Worship* (Phillipsburg, N.J.: Presbyterian & Reformed, 2001), 1–74.

The second Old Testament idea reflected in bin Laden's ideology is *ḥerem* warfare. *Ḥerem* may be compared to Islamic *jihad*, both of which have been roughly understood as "holy war." America was shocked when innocent civilians were killed in the terrorist acts of September 11, 2001. However, if we are honest readers of the Old Testament, is this so different from the slaughter of Canaanite men, women, and children prisoners of war that we read about in the book of Joshua?

The comparison raises a number of important issues with which we will deal in this essay. (1) How does *ḥerem* function within the Old Testament? (2) How does the God who ordered *ḥerem* relate to the God of the New Testament who sent his Son, Jesus Christ, not to kill people but rather to die for them? (3) In the light of our answers to the first two questions, how does this relate to the question that is perhaps the most important of all to the Christian: How are we to read the Old Testament in the light of the New Testament?

These questions are not simply theoretical; they are of the utmost importance for the practice of the church today. The church often finds itself at odds in terms of values and practice with the broader society.[2] This tension has sometimes been described as a culture war.[3] Indeed, some of evangelical Christianity's leading lights have used martial terminology to describe how the church should engage the world.[4] Some on the radical fringe of Christianity have even taken the next step and lifted up physical arms in order to defend the faith against encroachment.[5] As just one example, we can cite the 1993 shooting of an abortion doctor and his escort by Paul Hill, a defrocked Presbyterian minister. By his own testimony Mr. Hill believed he was doing the Lord's will in this shooting; in this he was supported by a small but vocal number of Christians.[6] It is only too easy to dismiss these people as Christianity's lunatic fringe, but

---

[2]I deal with this issue more broadly in *Daniel* (NIVAC; Grand Rapids: Zondervan, 1999).

[3]J. D. Hunter, *Culture Wars: The Struggle to Define America* (New York: Basic Books, 1991).

[4]F. A. Schaeffer, *A Christian Manifesto* (Westchester, Ill.: Crossway, 1981).

[5]J. Risen and J. L. Thomas, *Wrath of Angels: The American Abortion War* (New York: Basic Books, 1998).

[6]The recent HBO documentary "Soldiers in the Army of God" (which premiered on April 1, 2001) interviews a number of Hill's supporters.

can they legitimately appeal to the *herem* warfare of the Old Testament to justify their beliefs and practices?

On the other side, many Christians have disowned the Old Testament in order to avoid embracing the bloody acts of God that may be found in its pages. They note the tremendous difference between the God of Joshua on the one hand, and Jesus Christ on the other, who instructed us to love our enemies and to turn the other cheek. However, disregard for the Old Testament is only too convenient, and those who do so ignore the fact that the New Testament builds on the revelation of the Old Testament, both implicitly and explicitly affirming its message. Furthermore, as we will observe below, the New Testament in the final analysis is equally bloody as the Old Testament. It will not do simply to divorce the Old Testament from the canon and shape the God that we worship in the image of what we think is acceptable.

WHAT IS OLD TESTAMENT *HEREM* WARFARE?[7]

The term *herem* is notoriously hard to translate.[8] It may be translated "banned" or "devoted things." It refers to plundered items and people captured during the course of holy war. *Herem* involves consecration, the giving over of the captives of war to God.[9] Consecration is a word that suggests worship, and once we understand *herem* warfare in its whole context, we can see just how appropriate that understanding is. Thus, we will begin our exploration with a description of *herem* warfare in terms of three phases: what happens before, during, and after warfare.

---

[7]A much more extensive description of *herem* warfare may be found in Daniel G. Reid and Tremper Longman III, *God Is a Warrior* (Grand Rapids: Zondervan, 1995). Important bibliography includes F. Schwally, *Der heilige Krieg im alten Israel* (Leipzig: Dietrich, 1901); H. Fredriksson, *Jahwe als Kreiger: Studien zum alttestamentlichen Gottesbild* (Lund: Gleerup, 1945); Gerhard von Rad, *Holy War in Ancient Israel*, ed. and trans. Marva J. Dawn (Grand Rapids: Eerdmans, 1991); Rudolph Smend, *Yahweh War and Tribal Confederation* (Nashville: Abingdon, 1970); P. D. Miller Jr. *The Divine Warrior in Early Israel* (HSM 5; Cambridge, Mass.: Harvard Univ. Press, 1973). Three significant works by Mennonite scholars include John Howard Yoder, *The Original Revolution: Essays on Christian Pacifism* (Scottdale, Pa.: Herald, 1977); Millard C. Lind, *Yahweh Is a Warrior* (Scottdale, Pa.: Herald, 1980); and Vernard Eller, *War and Peace from Genesis to Revelation* (Scottdale, Pa.: Herald, 1981).

[8]See Philip D. Stern, *The Biblical Herem: A Window on Israel's Religious Experience* (BJS 211; Atlanta: Scholars Press, 1991).

[9]Note the discussion of the word by J. A. Naude, "חרם," *NIDOTTE*, 2:275–76.

The following synthesis is the result of studying the two holy-war law passages of Deuteronomy (chs. 7 and 20) as well as the many records of battles throughout the Old Testament.

Overarching Principle:
God Is Present with the Army in Battle

As we will see, at the heart of *herem* warfare is the presence of God with the army. Of course, where God is present, he must be worshiped, and thus we will not be surprised to see that *herem* is shaped largely by that fact. Indeed, it is not too strong to say that *herem* warfare is worship. The battlefield is sacred space. To be involved in warfare is a holy activity analogous to going to the temple.

Before Warfare

Seeking the will of God. God did not tell Israel that its enemies were his enemies. Quite the opposite is true, actually. Israel was to be an enemy to God's enemies. On a practical level, this meant that Israel had to know whether it was God's will that they go to war against a particular people. As we read the biblical battle accounts, we see that he made his will known to his people in one of two ways.

(1) The first way is illustrated by the battle of Jericho. As Joshua surveyed the future battlefield, he was confronted by a mysterious figure with "a drawn sword in his hand" (Josh. 5:13). This figure, who described himself as the "commander of the army of the LORD," is clearly Yahweh himself. After all, before what other person would Joshua fall "facedown to the ground in reverence" (Josh. 5:14)? It is at this time that God delivered the battle strategy to Joshua.

(2) The second way of discerning God's will was to actively seek it in the light of a tense circumstance. In 1 Samuel 23:1–6, David learned that the Philistines threatened the Judahite town of Keilah. Instead of rashly rushing to that city's defense, he rather "inquired of the LORD" (23:2). Though this story is set in the period when David was not yet king, he did have a priest in attendance (23:6), who would have used oracular means to find out what God wanted in this situation.

The importance of discovering God's will in the face of a potential enemy is underlined by the story in Joshua 9. Here a group of Gibeonites deceived Joshua into thinking they had come from a far country, though in reality they were from just down the road. As we will explain later, Deuteronomy 20 makes a distinction between how nations in the Promised Land were to be treated compared to those outside. Joshua made a rash decision that would come back to haunt Israel because "they did not inquire of the LORD" (Josh. 9:14).

Spiritual preparedness. When Israelites entered the sanctuary, they had to be spiritually prepared. In other words, they had to observe the purity laws of the Pentateuch. The same was true of the battlefield. Two stories illustrate the necessity of spiritual preparedness before engaging in *ḥerem* warfare.

When the Israelites emerged from their forty years of desert wandering, the second generation, born during the journey, had not, for unstated reasons, practiced circumcision. Thus, before engaging in *ḥerem* warfare in Canaan, the Israelite males were mass circumcised and, afterward, celebrated Passover (Josh. 5:2–12). This ceremony took place on the Jericho side of the Jordan within easy range of their enemies. Needless to say, it was dangerous to perform this operation on Israel's fighting men at this time. One need only remember what happened during Jacob's lifetime in the city of Shechem (Gen. 34). The implicit assumption of the passage in Joshua is that whatever the dangers from the nearby human enemies, it was far more horrific to imagine going into battle uncircumcised.

The other passage that illustrates our point comes from the time of David (2 Sam. 11). The passage begins with a not-so-subtle critique of David's staying home in Jerusalem in the spring "when kings go off to war" (2 Sam. 11:1). Soon, David got himself in trouble as a result of his apparent lack of activity. After a nap, he was strolling on the roof of his palace when he looked down and saw the naked Bathsheba taking a bath. Though fully aware that she was the wife of another man, he took her into his bed, and she became pregnant. Wishing to cover up his sin, David called her husband, Uriah the Hittite, back from the front lines on a pretense with the hope that he would sleep with her and believe the future birth was his child. David's scheme was frustrated by the fact that Uriah refused to sleep with his wife but chose to bed down that night "at the entrance to the palace with all his master's servants" (11:9).

What is of interest to us in our pursuit of an understanding of *herem* warfare is the response he gave the next day to David's bafflement at his actions: "The ark and Israel and Judah are staying in tents, and my master Joab and my lord's men are camped in the open fields. How could I go to my house to eat and drink and lie with my wife? As surely as you live, I will not do such a thing!" (11:11). In spite of David's continued efforts, Uriah resolutely refused to sleep with his wife.

The reason for this refusal is much deeper than typical warrior's bravado. "How can I enjoy myself when my comrades are miserable on the field?" If there was some of this in his refusal, that was not the underlying reason. Uriah's motivation may be found in Leviticus 15:11–18, which states that an emission of semen rendered a man unclean. If Uriah had had intercourse, he would have been temporarily unclean and thus not "battle ready." The striking contrast in 2 Samuel 11 pits David, the king after God's own heart, who here committed adultery and conspired to murder, against Uriah, a non-Israelite (Hittite) mercenary, who observed the fine points of the cultic code.

Sacrifice. The accounts of the ancient wars of Israel are selective. Not every action is recorded for every battle. We read about sacrifices before warfare on that occasion when it proved to be controversial. The following story, then, illustrates the practice of offering sacrifices before *herem* warfare, but elsewhere it was not reported because it happened without special incident.

In this case, Saul was the war leader, and his battle was against Israel's perennial enemy of the time, the Philistines (1 Sam. 13). In Saul's estimation, time was slipping away. The present was the optimal moment for the battle, and the issue was compounded by the desertion of troops who were waiting for the battle to commence. However, Saul well knew that sacrifices had to be offered before the conflict could begin, and the unstated assumption of the chapter is that only a priest like Samuel could legitimately offer sacrifices. But where was Samuel? He was supposed to be there already, but he was nowhere to be found. As a result, Saul finally gave in to his concerns and offered the sacrifices himself. When Samuel finally did arrive, he reviled Saul for his presumptuous act that demonstrated his lack of confidence in God the warrior, announcing that Saul's kingdom would "not endure" (13:14).

These prebattle sacrifices were motivated by the fact that the army would fight in the presence of God. Our next topic will make this fact more concrete.

The presence of the ark. Typical of early battle narratives is the role of the ark in the battle of Jericho (Josh. 6). God gave Joshua the instructions for how to wage the battle (5:2–5); central to the plan was the march around the city. For six days, the Israelites were to march around the city, and on the climactic seventh day they were to march around the city seven times. At the head of the army was the ark.

The ark was the mobile symbol of God's spiritual presence. The tabernacle, of course, was associated with God's presence, and its importance was due in large measure to the fact that it was the repository for the stationary ark. The most usual reason for the ark to depart the sanctuary was to accompany the army into battle and to serve as a sign of God's presence on the battlefield.

Described in Exodus 25:10–22, the ark was constructed from a rather simple design. It was a relatively small box, three and three-quarters feet long, two and a quarter feet wide, and two and a quarter feet high. It also had rings attached to the sides, through which poles were slid for carrying it. The importance of the ark in the battles of Israel may already be seen during the desert wanderings soon after its construction. These wanderings were, in essence, a long march into battle. We recognize this when we remember the language Moses used at the onset of a day's march. He would announce:

> Rise up, O LORD!
>> May your enemies be scattered;
>> may your foes flee before you. (Num. 10:35)

The presence of the ark represented God's participation in the battle. The only proper response when one is with God is worship. The Israelite soldier had to be spiritually prepared and offer sacrifices to God before the battle could begin.

> May the praise of God be in their mouths
>> and a double-edged sword in their hands,
> to inflict vengeance on the nations
>> and punishment on the peoples. (Ps. 149:6–7)

During the Battle

The march. With the presence of the ark we can see how the march into battle is a religious procession. Above we commented on how the ark led the Israelites through the desert and began the daily journey with a call for the divine warrior to rise up and scatter the enemies. A close reading of Numbers 2 indicates that when Israel camped during the march, the arrangement of the tribes resembled an ancient Near Eastern war camp. God, the warring king, had his tent in the middle, surrounded by his most devoted warriors, the Levites.[10] The rest of the tribes (army) were situated on all sides of the tent but beyond the Levites.

The religious nature of the march may also be observed in the role that the priests played. The priests, of course, carried the ark and thus were in the vanguard of the seven-day march around the city of Jericho. Later in Israelite history, in the context of Jehoshaphat's battles against the Moabites and Ammonites, we read a moving description of the final preparations and the march, which involved the Levites:

> Jehoshaphat bowed with his face to the ground, and all the people of Judah and Jerusalem fell down in worship before the LORD. Then some Levites from the Kohathites and Korahites stood up and praised the LORD, the God of Israel, with very loud voice.
>
> Early in the morning they left for the Desert of Tekoa. As they set out, Jehoshaphat stood and said, "Listen to me, Judah and people of Jerusalem! Have faith in the LORD your God and you will be upheld; have faith in his prophets and you will be successful." After consulting the people, Jehoshaphat appointed men to sing to the LORD and to praise him for the splendor of his holiness as they went out at the head of the army, saying:
>
> "Give thanks to the LORD,
>   for his love endures forever."
>
> As they began to sing and praise, the LORD set ambushes.... (2 Chron. 20:18–22)

---

[10]For the priests as God's bodyguards, see Tremper Longman, *Immanuel in Our Place: Seeing Christ in Israel's Worship* (Phillipsburg, N.J.: Presbyterian & Reformed, 2001), 139–50.

Prayer, religious song, and celebration all accompanied the waging of war in ancient Israel. Why? Because *herem* warfare was worship.

Warfare strategy. Perhaps the most interesting part of *herem* warfare has to do with warfare strategy. There is no simple formula to describe the war, and each battle recorded in the Old Testament has its unique characteristics. However, one common denominator runs through each successful battle: The victory is clearly the consequence of God's involvement in the battle. Human participation matters but is never determinative of the outcome. The people of God must fight, but great care is taken not to enter a battle with a superior force or with sophisticated weapons. Examples will help make this point.

During the period of the judges, God commissioned Gideon to rid the land of the Midianites, who had come to oppress at least a part of the land of Israel (Judg. 6–8). As Gideon prepared to meet the Midianites in battle from their camp near the spring of Harod, the Lord confronted him with a problem. He had too many warriors! Gideon then issued a command to relieve from duty those who were afraid. Twenty-two thousand went home, but still ten thousand remained. God then instructed Gideon to take those who remained down to the water to drink. Those who lapped with their hands to their mouths, three hundred men, were told to stay and fight the Midianites. Thus, the army was whittled down from thirty-two thousand to three hundred. Why go to such efforts not to enter a battle with too many soldiers? God himself provided the motivation: "in order that Israel may not boast against me that her own strength has saved her" (7:2).

The same may be seen in what may be called an individual *herem* war in the conflict between David and Goliath (1 Sam. 17). The context of the battle is Israel's conflict with the Philistines during the reign of King Saul. At this time, David was young, not even in the army, and was present at the battlefield only to bring provisions to his older brothers. The emphasis in the narrative is on David's youth and inexperience. While he was visiting the camp, the Philistines issued a challenge to Israel. They had a champion of unusual abilities and dimensions as well as great war experience in Goliath. Goliath kept challenging Israel to provide a champion of its own, but no one in the army had the courage to volunteer.

Finally, David passionately stepped forward to take on the arrogant infidel who defied "the armies of the living God" (1 Sam. 17:26). He entered the battle with no armor and only a simple slingshot. The contrast could not be more dramatic: a vulnerable and inexperienced youth versus a well-armored, experienced mercenary. David, however, was the easy victor in this well-known confrontation, and in his challenge to Goliath he expressed the heart of *ḥerem* warfare:

> David said to the Philistine, "You come against me with sword and spear and javelin, but I come against you in the name of the LORD Almighty, the God of the armies of Israel, whom you have defied. This day the LORD will hand you over to me, and I'll strike you down and cut off your head. Today I will give the carcasses of the Philistine army to the birds of the air and the beasts of the earth, and the whole world will know that there is a God in Israel. All those gathered here will know that it is not by sword or spear that the LORD saves; for the battle is the LORD's, and he will give all of you into our hands." (1 Sam. 17:45–47)

David fully understood that his victory was really God's victory. Nonetheless, we should take careful note of the fact that David had to act. He had to face Goliath and throw the stone that stunned him. He then had to take the sword and cut off the giant's head. Certainly God did not need him to do this since he was perfectly capable of destroying Goliath without David's involvement at all.

After the Battle

The march back. Of course, once the battle was completed, the army with the ark made the journey back to the sanctuary. This is likely the situation that is behind the liturgy in Psalm 24. After an assertion of God's sovereignty over his creation (24:1–2), verses 3–6 describe the type of person who may enter the sacred precincts. This may imply that someone or some group is seeking access to the sanctuary, and from verses 7–10 we suggest that it is the army that is in mind as they return to Jerusalem to place the ark back in the Most Holy Place.

Thus, we understand the conversation that takes place in 24:7–10 to be that between a Levitical gatekeeper and the priests who carry the ark at the head of the army. The first to speak are the latter, who demand access through the city gates:

> Lift up your heads, O you gates;
>> be lifted up, you ancient doors,
>> that the King of glory may come in. (Ps. 24:7)

The only possible way of understanding how God can be envisioned entering the gate of the city would be as represented by the ark. In any case, this request is followed by a response from the gatekeeper:

> Who is this King of glory? (Ps. 24:8a)

Now, of course, the priests knew full well who the King of glory was. But the question allowed for the descriptive praise of God the warrior. Again, the priests leading the army speak:

> The LORD strong and mighty,
>> the LORD mighty in battle.
> Lift up your heads, O you gates;
>> lift them up, you ancient doors,
>> that the King of glory may come in. (Ps. 24:8b–9)

This allows for an emphatic restatement of the question and answer:

> Who is he, this King of glory?
> The LORD Almighty—
>> he is the King of glory. (Ps. 24:10)

The celebration. Music played a key role in connection with *herem* warfare. We have seen how Jehoshaphat's army marched into battle singing hymns and how Psalm 24 was sung upon the return to the sacred precincts. Indeed, elsewhere I have shown how many psalms find their original setting before (Ps. 7), during (Ps. 91), and after (Ps. 24; 98) the waging of *herem* warfare.[11]

In terms of the last category, it is clearly the norm that hymns were sung in celebration of victory. After all, God had won the battle, so he deserved the praise. Many of the great

---

[11]Tremper Longman III, "Psalm 98: A Divine Warrior Victory Song," *JETS* 27 (1984): 125–31.

early poems of Israel were victory hymns for specific battles. Perhaps most remarkable is the Song of the Sea, sung on the occasion of the defeat of Egypt at the Re(e)d Sea. This is likely the earliest explicit mention of God as warrior:

> I will sing to the LORD,
>   for he is highly exalted.
> The horse and its rider
>   he has hurled into the sea.
> The LORD is my strength and my song;
>   he has become my salvation.
> He is my God, and I will praise him,
>   my father's God, and I will exalt him.
> The LORD is a warrior;
>   the LORD is his name.
> Pharaoh's chariots and his army
>   he has hurled into the sea. (Ex. 15:1–4b)

Another memorable occasion when music broke out as a result of victorious holy war was after Jephthah's victory against the Ammonites. In this case, however, the story comes to a sad end. It was Jephthah's daughter who first came out of the house "dancing to the sound of tambourines" (Judg. 11:34); in fulfillment of a vow, her father had to reluctantly dedicate her as a "whole-burnt sacrifice" (Heb. ʿolah) to the Lord.

The ḥerem. We have been using *ḥerem* as a term to describe the waging of war in Israel, in essence as a synonym for holy war or Yahweh war. In actuality, *ḥerem* refers to the climactic aspect of divine warfare: the offering of the conquered people and their possessions to the Lord.

(1) We must point out once again that *ḥerem* indicates that warfare is worship in the Old Testament. God won the victory, so he was due the spoils. The biblical account is not strictly consistent on this account,[12] but what this typically meant for the plunder is that it was turned over to the priestly establishment for their use or distribution. In terms of the prisoners of war and the captured citizens of an enemy town, it meant only one thing: death. The principle behind the latter practice appears to be that because they were unclean, these ungodly people brought into the presence of God had to be destroyed.

---

[12]1 Samuel 30:16–26 appears to be an exception to the following rule.

(2) Deuteronomy 20:10–18 makes a clear distinction between battles fought outside the Promised Land and those waged "in the cities of the nations the LORD your God is giving you as an inheritance." The full text describing the fate of the latter group is instructive. After saying that the cities outside of the Promised Land could be given the opportunity to surrender and thus be subject to servitude, God commanded that Israel

> not leave alive anything that breathes. Completely destroy them—the Hittites, Amorites, Canaanites, Perizzites, Hivites and Jebusites—as the LORD your God has commanded you. Otherwise, they will teach you to follow all the detestable things they do in worshiping their gods, and you will sin against the LORD your God. (Deut. 20:16–18)

The two opening battle accounts of the Conquest illustrate the importance of keeping *herem*. After the battle of Jericho and after separating Rahab from the group, "they devoted [*hrm*] the city to the LORD and destroyed with the sword every living thing in it—men and women, young and old, cattle, sheep and donkeys" (Josh. 6:21). Thus ended the most powerful city within Palestine at the time.

The next battle was against puny Ai, whose very name means "ruin." Even so, as a force of Israelites moved against Ai, they were repulsed. Joshua was shaken to the core by this turn of events. Inquiring of the Lord, he discovered that someone had not observed *herem* after Jericho. Through divine guidance, they discovered that Achan had stolen some of the plunder and did not turn it over to the Lord. Once the sin was dealt with, the Israelites returned to Ai, and this time the conflict came to a successful conclusion.

Jericho and Ai thus serve as a didactic statement and warning about the importance of keeping *herem*. Obedience brings victory against the toughest opponents, while disobedience means defeat even against the weakest.

In conclusion, we must point out that the Bible does not understand the destruction of the men, women, and children of these cities as a slaughter of innocents. Not even the children are considered innocent. They are all part of an inherently wicked culture that, if allowed to live, would morally and theologically pollute the people of Israel. The passage in Joshua 6 quoted above was prefaced by the motivation to avoid their own destruction. Indeed, from the perspective of the Bible, God had practiced great patience with the people who lived in Palestine. The reason why the descendents of Abraham had to wait so long before entering the Promised Land was because "the sin of the Amorites has not yet reached its full measure" (Gen. 15:16).

HOW DOES THE GOD WHO ORDERED *ḤEREM* RELATE TO THE GOD OF THE NEW TESTAMENT?

Many people would pit the above picture of a violent God who destroys his enemies against the New Testament understanding of God as a God of love who sends his Son to the cross to die for evil people. To be sure, Jesus even tells his disciples (and through them the church) to "put your sword back in its place" (Matt. 26:52). However, quoting from the book of Revelation immediately belies such a simplistic view of the Bible. No more fearful picture of a vengeful, violent God may be found than that described in Revelation 20:11–15:

> Then I saw a great white throne and him who was seated on it. Earth and sky fled from his presence, and there was no place for them. And I saw the dead, great and small, standing before the throne, and books were opened. Another book was opened, which is the book of life. The dead were judged according to what they had done as recorded in the books. The sea gave up the dead that were in it, and death and Hades gave up the dead that were in them, and each person was judged according to what he had done. Then death and Hades were thrown into the lake of fire. The lake of fire is the second death. If anyone's name was not found written in the book of life, he was thrown into the lake of fire.

How does the Old Testament relate to the New Testament? We find it helpful to answer this question by describing what might be called five phases of holy war in the Bible.

Phase 1: God Fights the Flesh-and-Blood Enemies of Israel

We do not have to dwell long on this phase, because this is the type of *herem* warfare that we have been describing in the earlier part of this chapter. The list of battles is long, and we have already cited parts of a number of them, but here we would include Jericho, the wars against the southern coalition of Canaanite kings, and the wars against the northern coalition. God fought on behalf of many of the judges as well as faithful kings such as David and Jehoshaphat. Indeed, at times God even used foreign nations to fight against Israel's enemies in a way that helped his people. In the latter instance, we think of the prophet Nahum, who announced the appearance of the divine warrior who would fight (in this case through the Babylonians) against Israel's long-time oppressor, Assyria.[13]

Phase 2: God Fights Israel

It would be wrong to say that "God was on Israel's side" pure and simple. Israel's election was not a carte blanche to wage war against anyone at any time. It should be clear by now that God used Israel as an instrument of his judgment against evil, oppressive nations. This raises the question of what would happen when the nation of Israel itself turned against God and committed evil acts.[14]

The answer to this question may be found in the form of the covenant itself, and here we see the connection between covenant theology and *herem* warfare. As has been well established, the covenant is a legal-political metaphor of God's relationship with his people.[15] The great king Yahweh makes a treaty with his vassal people, Israel. In this arrangement, Yahweh promises to be their God and protect them, and Israel promises to be his people and obey the law he has given them. In the covenant treaty, the law is backed up by sanctions: Blessings

---

[13]See Tremper Longman III, "Nahum," in *The Minor Prophets*, ed. T. E. McComiskey (Grand Rapids: Eerdmans, 1993), 2:765–829.

[14]W. L. Moran, "The End of the Unholy War and the Anti-Exodus," *Bib* 44 (1963): 333–42.

[15]Meredith G. Kline, *Treaty of the Great King* (Grand Rapids: Eerdmans, 1963); D. J. McCarthy, *Old Testament Covenant: A Survey of Recent Opinions*, 2d ed. (Rome: Pontifical Biblical Institute, 1978).

flow from obedience and curses for disobedience. The book of Deuteronomy, a covenant renewal of the relationship established at Sinai, is particularly expansive with its blessings and curses. Many of them have to do with military success and failure. Illustrative is the following pair, the first contingent on obedience and the second the result of disobedience:

> The LORD will grant that the enemies who rise up against you will be defeated before you. They will come at you from one direction but flee from you in seven. (Deut. 28:7)

> The LORD will cause you to be defeated before your enemies. You will come at them from one direction but flee from them in seven, and you will become a thing of horror to all the kingdoms on earth. (Deut. 28:25)

The history of Israel has many examples of the outworking of these covenant curses. We have already observed one in the discussion of postbattle *ḥerem*, namely, Ai. A second example surrounds the defeat of the Israelites at the hands of the Philistines at the end of the reign of Eli (1 Sam. 4–6). The text describes Eli as good-hearted but incompetent. He was particularly incompetent as a father, and his two sons, Hophni and Phinehas, were evil men, who were also in charge of Israel's army.

In an initial encounter with the Philistines, the Israelites were soundly defeated, losing about four thousand men. Hophni and Phinehas then realized that their mistake was in forgetting to bring the ark onto the battlefield. From their actions as well as the consequences, it appears that this realization came about not because of any deeply held faith in God but rather from the misconception that the ark was like a magical box by which God's presence and power could be manipulated.

The two brothers then sent for the ark, which arrived in the war camp before the second confrontation with the Philistines. God's reputation as a warrior apparently preceded this act, because the Philistines were visibly shaken by the news that the ark was now in the possession of the Israelite army. Nonetheless, they gathered their courage and engaged the Israelites. The Israelites were soundly defeated, Hophni and Phinehas were killed, and perhaps most terrible of all, the ark was captured and taken by the Philistines.

That God was able but unwilling to save the Israelites on that day becomes clear in the aftermath of the battle. The Philistines followed typical ancient Near Eastern custom and moved the captured ark into the temple of their chief god, Dagon. This act demonstrated their acknowledgment that Yahweh was a god, but one who was inferior to their god. The next day, however, events belied this belief when they discovered the statue of Dagon flat on its face before the ark, as if in worship. After they hoisted the statue to an upright position, the same thing happened the next day. Finally, they got the message. The Israelites were defeated not because of God's inability but because he had determined to defeat the Israelites as judgment for their sin.

Our next example is a climactic moment in the history of Israel, namely, the Babylonian defeat of Jerusalem followed by the Exile. Though only a small portion of the Old Testament actually narrates the destruction of Jerusalem and the exile, close analysis reveals that a number of books offer a theological rationale for it. Many scholars, for instance, are convinced that the final redaction of Samuel–Kings, if not also Joshua and Judges, took place during the Exile and provided a rationale for these horrific events. These books helped answer the question why the people of God were defeated and sent into exile. It was not because Babylon was a stronger nation but because God used this pagan nation, unwitting to be sure, as an instrument of his judgment.

The first few verses of Daniel are a case in point (Dan. 1:1–3). The events of these verses purport to have taken place in 605 B.C. and thus would be the first time that Nebuchadnezzar exerted pressure against Judah. He was successful in reducing them to a form of vassal status, indicated by taking hostage sacred objects from the temple and a token of the youth of the noble class. However, these verses give a deeper meaning to the events than would have been recognizable on the surface. It is not that Nebuchadnezzar was so powerful but rather because God gave Jehoiakim into his hand.

The one book that reflects on the destruction of Jerusalem from a theological and emotional perspective is the book of Lamentations. This book is filled with talk of the divine warrior, but in this case the warrior was not protecting his people—he appeared as their enemy:

> The Lord is like an enemy;
>> he has swallowed up Israel.
> He has swallowed up all her palaces
>> and destroyed her strongholds.
> He has multiplied mourning and lamentation
>> for the Daughter of Judah. (Lam. 2:5)

Thus, from these accounts it is clear that God was not for Israel without question but would come as a warrior against his people when they disobeyed. The Exile was a dramatic expression of this second phase. However, it was not definitive. Indeed, it is not even the last statement of *ḥerem* warfare in the Old Testament.

Phase 3: God Will Come in the Future As Warrior

God did not allow his people to come to an end in the Exile. Though probably connected to the exile of the northern kingdom in 722 B.C., the following oracle of Hosea expresses God's unwillingness to completely give up on his people:

> How can I give you up, Ephraim?
>> How can I hand you over, Israel?
> How can I treat you like Admah?
>> How can I make you like Zeboiim?
> My heart is changed within me;
>> all my compassion is aroused.
> I will not carry out my fierce anger,
>> nor will I turn and devastate Ephraim.
> For I am God, and not man—
>> the Holy One among you.
> I will not come in wrath. (Hos. 11:8–9)

In the light of this we may not be surprised to discover that one of the dominant themes of the postexilic prophets was the future appearance of the divine warrior, who would free his people from their present oppressors.

Daniel 7 is a good example. This chapter may be divided into two parts: Daniel's vision (7:1–14) and the angelic interpretation of that vision (7:15–28). In this retelling of the vision, we will combine the two. The vision itself may be divided into two parts by virtue of the setting. The first part is set on the earth, specifically at the coastline of a turbulent sea. By the time of Daniel, the sea was a well-established symbol for those forces ranged against God and his created order. This symbolic value for the sea goes back to ancient Near Eastern myths, such as the Babylonian *Enuma Elish* and the Ugaritic Baal myth.[16] In other words, the very setting of the vision elicits horror.

Out of this chaotic sea come four beasts. The first is a hybrid animal: part eagle, part lion, part human. The very fact that this is an animal of mixed essence would also have made the Israelite reader uneasy; it was an offense to creation order. The following beasts are of similar threatening appearance. The fourth is beyond description, with only its metallic teeth and destroying claws being described. From this fourth beast come ten horns, and Daniel's description ultimately focuses on one boastful horn. This part of the vision describes those evil human kingdoms that oppress God's people.

In verses 9–14, the scene shifts. We are now in the divine throne room, and God is the Ancient of Days, who sits to render judgment on these beasts. Into his presence comes a humanlike figure riding a cloud. Like the sea, cloud-riding is also a well-established symbol, in this case for the warrior God. We can only speculate how Daniel's original audience understood how God could appear before God (see below for the use of this passage in the New Testament). In any case, this figure, along with the saints of the Most High, destroys the beasts' grip on God's people.

This is the note on which the Old Testament closes. It is a hopeful message: One day God will come again and free them from their oppression.

Phase 4: Jesus Christ Fights
the Spiritual Powers and Authorities

The first voice we hear in the New Testament is that of John the Baptist, sounding remarkably like the Old Testament prophets of phase 3:

---

[16]M. K. Wakeman, *God's Battle with the Monster: A Study in Biblical Imagery* (Leiden: Brill, 1973); J. Day, *God's Conflict with the Dragon and the Sea* (Cambridge: Cambridge Univ. Press, 1975); C. Kloos, *Yhwh's Combat with the Sea: A Canaanite Tradition in the Religion of Ancient Israel* (Leiden: Brill, 1986).

> You brood of vipers! Who warned you to flee from the coming wrath? Produce fruit in keeping with repentance. And do not think you can say to yourselves, "We have Abraham as our father." I tell you that out of these stones God can raise up children for Abraham. The ax is already at the root of the trees, and every tree that does not produce good fruit will be cut down and thrown into the fire. (Matt. 3:7–10; see also vv. 11–12)

John expects that the one coming after him will fill the role of the violent warrior who will rid the land of its oppressors. Imagine his shock later when the one he does recognize through baptism preaches the good news, heals the sick, and exorcises demons. As a matter of fact, we have a record of his reaction in Matthew 11:1–19. John is now in prison and hears reports about Jesus' ministry. His doubts lead him to send two of his disciples to Jesus to ask the skeptical question: "Are you the one who was to come, or should we expect someone else?" (11:2).

> Jesus replied, "Go back and report to John what you hear and see: The blind receive sight, the lame walk, those who have leprosy are cured, the deaf hear, the dead are raised, and the good news is preached to the poor. Blessed is the man who does not fall away on account of me." (Matt. 11:4–6)

Through his actions, Jesus informs John that he has in fact chosen the right person. However, Jesus is also subtly changing—indeed, enriching—John's understanding of his mission. In a nutshell, Jesus is the divine warrior, but he has intensified and heightened the battle. No longer is the battle a physical battle against flesh-and-blood enemies, but rather it is directed toward the spiritual powers and authorities. Furthermore, this battle is fought with nonphysical weapons.

The exorcisms of the New Testament are a case in point. Here we see the violent nature of the conflict. Matthew 8:28–34 (see also Mark 5:1–20; Luke 8:26–39) narrates the story of Jesus' ordering the demons in two demon-possessed men to enter into pigs, which then throw themselves into a lake and are destroyed.

The climax of phase 4 is violent but in an ironic way. Paul looks back on the crucifixion and pronounces it a military victory over the demonic realm:

> When you were dead in your sins and in the uncircumcision of your sinful nature, God made you alive with Christ. He forgave us all our sins, having canceled the written code, with its regulations, that was against us and that stood opposed to us; he took it away, nailing it to the cross. And having disarmed the powers and authorities, he made a public spectacle of them, triumphing over them by the cross. (Col. 2:13–15)

Jesus' ascension into heaven is also described in military language, indeed by the citation of a holy-war hymn from the Old Testament, Psalm 68:

> But to each one of us grace has been given as Christ apportioned it. This is why it says:
>
> "When he ascended on high,
>   he led captives in his train
>   and gave gifts to men." (Eph. 4:8)

Jesus defeated the powers and authorities, not by killing but by dying!

Indeed, the transition from the old way of physical warfare to the new era of spiritual warfare was dramatically illustrated by the scene in the Garden of Gethsemane. As Jesus was being arrested, Peter, always impetuous, grabbed a sword and chopped off the ear of the high priest's servant (Matt. 26:47–56; Mark 14:43–52; Luke 22:47–53; John 18:1–11). Jesus then declared:

> Put your sword back in its place ... for all who draw the sword will die by the sword. Do you think I cannot call on my Father, and he will at once put at my disposal more than twelve legions of angels? But how then would the Scriptures be fulfilled that say it must happen in this way? (Matt. 26:52–54)

When Jesus told Peter to put away the sword, he was telling the church that would follow that physical violence could not be used to further his cause.[17] The object of Christ's warfare is spiritual, not physical, and the weapons used are spiritual, not physical (see comments below on Eph. 6).

---

[17]In my opinion, this does not settle the debate between just-war advocates and pacifists. It only declares that wars in the name of Christianity are not legitimate.

Phase 5: The Final Battle

Does this mean that John the Baptist was wrong? As it turns out, he was not, but like a typical prophet, he did not have a clear sense of how his prophecy would work out (1 Peter 1:10–12).[18] According to the fuller revelation of the New Testament, Jesus' first coming was not the end of the story. He will come again, as warrior. Jesus himself cites Daniel 7:13 (Mark 13:26; Rev. 1:7) and describes his future return riding on the clouds. In our examination of Daniel 7 above, we indicated that the cloud is the divine war-chariot. When Jesus returns again, he will complete the victory assured by his death on the cross. Of the many passages in the apocalyptic portions of the New Testament that could be chosen as an example, Revelation 19:11–21 is among the most graphic:

> I saw heaven standing open and there before me was a white horse, whose rider is called Faithful and True. With justice he judges and makes war. His eyes are like blazing fire, and on his head are many crowns. He has a name written on him that no one knows but he himself. He is dressed in a robe dipped in blood, and his name is the Word of God. The armies of heaven were following him, riding on white horses and dressed in fine linen, white and clean. Out of his mouth comes a sharp sword with which to strike down the nations. "He will rule them with an iron scepter." He treads the winepress of the fury of the wrath of God Almighty. On his robe and on his thigh he has this name written:
>
> KING OF KINGS AND LORD OF LORDS
>
> And I saw an angel standing in the sun, who cried in a loud voice to all the birds flying in midair, "Come, gather together for the great supper of God, so that you may eat the flesh of kings, generals, and mighty men, of horses and their riders, and the flesh of all people, free and slave, small and great."
>
> Then I saw the beast and the kings of the earth and their armies gathered together to make war against the rider on the horse and his army. But the beast was captured, and with him the false prophet who had performed

---

[18]On my understanding of the workings of prophecy, see my *Reading the Bible with Heart and Mind* (Colorado Springs: NavPress, 1997), 163–79.

the miraculous signs on his behalf. With these signs he had deluded those who had received the mark of the beast and worshiped his image. The two of them were thrown alive into the fiery lake of burning sulfur. The rest of them were killed with the sword that came out of the mouth of the rider on the horse, and all the birds gorged themselves on their flesh.

We quote this passage at length to communicate the violence associated with the Second Coming. In essence, we are reading a highly symbolic description of the final judgment. This terrifying conclusion to history is, in actuality, good news to the oppressed people of God to whom the book of Revelation is addressed.

The passage is clear in terms of showing the violent nature of the return of Jesus, the warrior. However, we would like to make two additional points. (1) This description of Jesus is built in large out of passages from Deuteronomy, Psalms, and Isaiah, passages that describe Yahweh as the divine warrior. (2) The description of Jesus here contrasts with the enemy, the unholy warrior known as the beast in Revelation 13:1–10.

FROM THE CANAANITES TO SATAN HIMSELF: CONTINUITY AND DISCONTINUITY IN HEREM WARFARE

With a background on Old Testament *herem* warfare and a survey of its practice from the Old Testament into the New, we are well prepared to explore the question of the relationship between the Testaments. First, however, we must make some *general* comments about the relationship between the Testaments.

It appears obvious that there is continuity between Old and New Testaments. Jesus twice gives what is essentially a lesson in hermeneutics when, after his resurrection, he appears to two different groups of disciples. (1) He speaks to two disciples who have yet to recognize their resurrected Lord:

> "How foolish you are, and how slow of heart to believe all that the prophets have spoken! Did not the Christ have to suffer these things and then enter his glory?" And beginning with Moses and all the Prophets, he explained to them what was said in all the Scriptures concerning himself. (Luke 24:25–27)

"All the Scriptures," "Moses and all the Prophets"—by which is meant the entire Old Testament—anticipate the coming suffering and glorification of Christ.

(2) This same theme is underlined when Jesus soon speaks to a broader group of disciples and declares:

> This is what I told you while I was still with you: Everything must be fulfilled that is written about me in the Law of Moses, the Prophets and the Psalms. (Luke 24:44)

No wonder so much of the New Testament looks back and cites the Old Testament. Augustine was surely correct when he famously said: "The New is in the Old Testament concealed; the Old is in the New revealed."

As we go back to the Old Testament, we must admit that the way Jesus fulfills the Old Testament is not always obvious. Of course, there is enough that was clear that people like John the Baptist had messianic expectations, but as we have already seen in reference to John, he was surprised by the form that the fulfillment took.

I have found helpful an analogy with a detective novel. A detective novel is filled with hints and clues pointing to the one who committed the crime. In a well-written example of this genre, however, readers will not be sure who the culprit is until it is revealed by the expert sleuth at the end. However, if one were to go back to read the beginning again, it would be with a fuller understanding. All the clues and hints would make more sense in the light of the knowledge of the end. One could never read the beginning of the story quite the same, and this holds true for the Christian reader of the Old Testament, who now knows the surprising end of the story.

The surprise element of the fulfillment also imparts a sense of discontinuity as well as continuity. In some cases, the fulfillment radically changes the practice of God's people. When Jesus offered himself as a once-and-for-all sacrifice on the cross, it does not mean that sacrifice is no longer a crucial theological category, but it does mean that Christians no longer offer animal sacrifices.

I argue that there is both continuity and discontinuity between the Old and New Testaments on the issue of *herem* warfare. The God of the Old Testament is not a different God from the God we encounter in the New Testament. Nor did God change his mind. The war against the Canaanites was simply an earlier phase of the battle that comes to its climax on the cross and its completion at the final judgment. The object of warfare moves from the Canaanites, who are the object of God's wrath for their sin, to the spiritual powers and principalities, and then finally to the utter destruction of all evil, human and spiritual.

Indeed, it must be said that those who have moral difficulties with the genocide in the conquest of Canaan should have even more serious difficulties with the final judgment. In the latter, all those who do not follow Christ—men, women, and children—will be thrown into the lake of fire. The alternatives to embracing this picture are either rejecting the biblical God or playing the Marcionite game of choosing those Scriptures that suit us, or perhaps treating the final judgment as a metaphor for total annihilation. However, even the latter is not a pleasant thought and still raises issues about how a loving God can exercise any kind of penalty toward the wicked.

A number of years ago Meredith Kline, a brilliant Old Testament theologian whose writings have unfortunately been neglected, introduced the concept of intrusion ethics into the discussion of *herem* warfare.[19] Kline reminds us that the punishment for sin is death. The lesson that rebellion—and all sin is rebellion—leads to death is made clear in the Garden of Eden (Gen. 2:17). It is only because of God's extraordinary grace that Adam and Eve were not killed on the spot when they ate the fruit of the tree. Indeed, it is because of that grace that *any of us* breathe. The period of God's extraordinary grace, often called common grace, is a special circumstance. In this light, we should not be amazed that God ordered the death of the Canaanites, but rather we should stand in amazement *that he lets anyone live*. The Conquest, according to Kline, involves the intrusion of the ethics of the end times, the consummation, into the period of common grace. In a sense, the destruction of the Canaanites is a preview of the final judgment.

Of course, we are left with disturbing questions. Why the Canaanites? Why not some other people? Are the Canaanites really extraordinarily evil? While perhaps the case can be made from their own texts that the Canaanites were evil, I do not think it can be shown that they were more evil than the Assyrians or

---

[19]The discussion may be found in his book, *The Structure of Biblical Authority* (Grand Rapids: Eerdmans, 1972).

the Israelites themselves. Here, like Job, we are left unanswered as to why suffering comes to one and not another.

Even so, the Bible makes it clear that we are still involved in *ḥerem* warfare; but rather than being directed toward physical enemies, it is a spiritual battle. Ephesians 6:10–18 is a programmatic statement in this regard:

> Finally, be strong in the Lord and in his mighty power. Put on the full armor of God so that you can take your stand against the devil's schemes. For our struggle is not against flesh and blood, but against the rulers, against the authorities, against the powers of this dark world and against the spiritual forces of evil in the heavenly realms. Therefore put on the full armor of God, so that when the day of evil comes, you may be able to stand your ground, and after you have done everything, to stand. Stand firm then, with the belt of truth buckled around your waist, with the breastplate of righteousness in place, and with your feet fitted with the readiness that comes from the gospel of peace. In addition to all this, take up the shield of faith, with which you can extinguish all the flaming arrows of the evil one. Take the helmet of salvation and the sword of the Spirit, which is the word of God. And pray in the Spirit on all occasions with all kinds of prayers and requests. With this in mind, be alert and always keep on praying for all the saints.

Here we see that the church is commanded to join in the struggle against the spiritual enemies of God. We also can see that the weapons employed in such a battle are spiritual, not physical (i.e., truth, righteousness, and so on).[20]

Though this is a programmatic statement, attention to this theme reveals that there are many passages that use military language to describe the Christian's spiritual battle in the world. Interestingly, war language is associated with the spiritual struggle that goes on within our own hearts and minds:[21]

---

[20]See the development of this idea in Dan Allender and Tremper Longman III, *Bold Love* (Colorado Springs: NavPress, 1991).

[21]Interestingly, some Muslim clerics also speak of a transition from a physical *jihad* to a spiritual one, in which the battle goes on in the heart and mind of the individual believer. This seems to be based on a wide use of the term *jihad* in the Qur'an and also in the Hadith.

For though we live in the world, we do not wage war as the world does. The weapons we fight with are not the weapons of the world. On the contrary, they have divine power to demolish strongholds. We demolish arguments and every pretension that sets itself up against the knowledge of God, and we take captive every thought to make it obedient to Christ. (2 Cor. 10:3–5)

CONCLUSION

In conclusion, we can see discontinuity between the Old and New Testaments in regard to the topic of *herem* warfare. While in the Old Testament the Israelites were often used by God as an instrument of his judgment, it is now a betrayal of the gospel to take up arms to defend or promote the interests of Christ.

However, this discontinuity is not absolute. There is also continuity, especially as we look to the New Testament's picture of the final judgment. In addition, though it is not a main theme, the Old Testament prophets sometimes draw the curtains back and allow the reader to see the spiritual battle that has been waged throughout history.[22] Indeed, all *herem* warfare, spiritual and physical, derives from the conflict anticipated in the curse against the serpent at the time of the Fall:

> I will put enmity
>> between you and the woman,
>> and between your offspring and hers;
> he will crush your head,
>> and you will strike his heel. (Gen. 3:15)

---

[22]Daniel 10 discusses the spiritual battle behind the battle between nations as a conflict of the (angelic) princes of Persia, Greece, and Israel. See Longman, *Daniel*, 244–66.

RESPONSES TO
TREMPER LONGMAN III

A RESPONSE TO
TREMPER LONGMAN III

C. S. Cowles

We are indebted to Tremper Longman III for cutting through the abstraction that inevitably attends our discussion of events that occurred three millennia ago and for putting a human face on Canaanite genocide. It is not the face of Jesus but of Osama bin Laden.

Longman begins his essay by noting, with considerable justification, that Osama is someone whose terrorist attacks were entirely in harmony with "the slaughter of Canaanite men, women, and children prisoners of war that we read about in the book of Joshua." The parallels are striking and sobering. Both believed that "sacred space" had been occupied by "infidels." Both were convinced that their genocidal "holy war" had been ordained and blessed by God. Both were intent on destroying the enemy down to the last crippled grandmother and mentally retarded child. Longman does not commend Osama, but neither does he condemn him, much less express outrage over his murderous acts. To do so would be, by implication, to condemn and disown the wanton destruction of human life in the land of Canaan.

Thus, Longman leaves us with no illusions as to what *herem* is about or the theological assumptions behind it. *Herem* is a carefully crafted and highly ritualized ideology of death and destruction. It gives divine sanction for people of one race and religion to dehumanize and demonize people of another race and religion, thereby justifying their total destruction. It fits the classic definition of evil: It "destroys and does not build up; it rips and it does not mend; it cuts and it does not bind. It strives always and everywhere to annihilate."[1] It strikes at the very heart of Christian faith in areas that cry out for a response.

The character of God. Martin Luther asked Erasmus rhetorically, "When you take Christ out of the Bible, what have you left?"[2] By isolating, identifying, and naming the various strands of divine commands and actions in reference to Canaanite genocide, Longman shows us what we have left. It is a definitive and chilling portrait of a God who is ontologically violent.[3] He is a God who conceived, commanded, and commended the indiscriminate and wanton slaughter of the Canaanites and whose "presence" is "at the heart of *herem* warfare." He is a God for whom "*herem* warfare is worship" and "the battlefield . . . sacred space." He loathes "enemies" and wills their total destruction. He is so determined to destroy the Canaanites that he "hardened their hearts . . . so that he might destroy them totally, exterminating them without mercy" (Josh. 11:20). He made sure they didn't have a chance.

When you take God incarnate in the historical Jesus out of the picture, what you have left is a God more concerned about ritual purity than the lives of human beings, a God for whom *herem* is not only the essence of Yahweh war but its "climactic aspect," and "the vanquished enemies become . . . a [human] sacrifice, something 'devoted to God.'"[4] Yahweh is a God who does not consider the killing of children as "a slaughter of innocents," since "not even the children are considered innocent" but "are part of an inherently wicked culture."[5] He is so destructive in his malignant wrath that if he lets anyone live, that is "a special circumstance," an "extraordinary grace." He is, in reference to

---

[1]Jeffrey Russell, *Mephistopheles: The Devil in the Modern World* (Ithaca, N.Y.: Cornell Univ. Press, 1986), 23.

[2]As cited in Willem Jan Kooiman, *Luther and the Bible,* trans. John Schmidt (Philadelphia: Muhlenberg, 1961), 208.

[3]After citing Isa. 13:4–9, Daniel G. Reid and Tremper Longman III begin their article, "When God Declares War," with this statement: "Isaiah won't let us escape the fact that our God is violent. In fact, Scripture often describes him as a warrior, a warring king who obliterates his enemies" (*Christianity Today* [Oct. 28, 1996], 14).

[4]Ibid., 17.

[5]Ibid, 14–15.

genocidal violence, more demonic than Satan.[6] If this is what God is like—a God whose image is reflected in Osama bin Laden—we can surely understand theologian Walter Wink when he protests, "Against such an image of God the revolt of atheism is an act of pure religion."[7]

The character of Christ. It is not that Christ has been literally taken "out of the Bible" in Longman's construal, but the "Prince of Peace" (Isa. 9:6) has been recast as a "divine warrior" in the image of Yahweh, the genocidal warrior of the Old Testament. True, "no longer is the battle a physical battle against flesh-and-blood enemies, but rather it is directed toward the spiritual powers and authorities." Lest we imagine that this signaled a fundamental change in God's character or battle strategy, Longman hurries on to point us to the book of Revelation, where "no more fearful picture of a vengeful, violent God may be found." The Apocalypse clearly shows "the violent nature of the return of Jesus, the warrior."

Thus, the center of gravity in Longman's Christology moves from the Gospels to the Apocalypse. By interpreting its highly symbolic language literally, the nonviolent Jesus of the Gospels is transformed into a violent warrior. This enables Longman to erase the fundamental discontinuity between the God of Joshua and the God of Jesus and tie together Canaanite genocide and the final judgment.[8] Thus, like Clark Kent emerging from the telephone booth as Superman, Jesus at his return will cast aside his servant garments and will disclose who he really is: a fierce, merciless, and physically violent eschatological terminator who will make the blood of his enemies flow knee-deep as in the days of Joshua. Having failed to reconcile the world to the Father through the power of Calvary's love, he will come again as a "violent . . . warrior" and will smash his enemies into oblivion after the manner of earthly kings, tyrants, and warmongers.

To say that this radical reconfiguration of Jesus rips the very heart out of the gospel is an understatement. We might ask: Does it represent sound hermeneutical practice to use the Apocalypse,

---

[6]Nowhere in Scripture is *ḥerem* or any genocidal activity attributed to Satan.

[7]Walter Wink, *Engaging the Powers* (Minneapolis: Fortress, 1992), 149.

[8]See a critique of this connection between Canaanite genocide and the eschaton in my response to Daniel L. Gard's essay.

with its notoriously slippery and unfathomable language, to marginalize and thus empty the apostolic witness to a nonviolent Christ of its radical content? Are we to trade off the Word who "became flesh and made his dwelling among us" (John 1:14) for the often-violent and sometimes contradictory imagery of the New Testament's most enigmatic book?[9]

Are we to believe that Jesus was mistaken when he grounded his command to "love your enemies" in the character of God, whom he claimed "causes his sun to rise on the evil and the good, and sends rain on the righteous and the unrighteous" (Matt. 5:44–45)? Are we to doubt the veracity of his categorical statement that God "is kind to the ungrateful and wicked" (Luke 6:35)? Was he being hypocritical in telling us to be merciful and to "put your sword back in its place" (Matt. 26:52), when he had no intention of doing the same in the eschaton? Are we to dismiss as "simplistic" the "New Testament understanding of God as a God of love who sends his Son to the cross to die for evil people"? Can we pigeonhole the earthly ministry of Jesus as at best an interim phase and at worst flawed and even fraudulent in its revelatory content? Would Paul have been closer to expressing who Jesus really was if he had said to the Corinthians, "For I resolved to know nothing while I was with you except Jesus Christ as divine warrior" instead of Christ "crucified" (1 Cor. 2:2)?

Interpreting the Scriptures. There is another way of forming our understanding of God: It is to come to the Scriptures by way of the portrait of Jesus that is rooted and anchored in the Gospels and New Testament letters. It is to see, as Luther did, Christ as the "'central point of the circle' around which everything else in the Bible revolves."[10] It is to read the Scriptures not from beginning to end but from the incarnate Christ

---

[9]J. Denny Weaver's analysis of the book of Revelation concludes that "the slain lamb indicates a nonviolent confrontation between reign of God and reign of evil, and a nonviolent victory via death and resurrection for the reign of God.... It is by proclamation of the Word, not by armies and military might, that God's judgment occurs.... The God of dispensationalism is a violent and vengeful god who overcomes evil and violence with greater violence. The God of Revelation is a God who overcomes nonviolently through the Word, which is Jesus Christ" (*The Nonviolent Atonement* [Grand Rapids: Eerdmans, 2001], 32–33, and n.29).

[10]Cited in Jack B. Rogers and Donald K. McKim, *The Authority and Interpretation of the Bible* (San Francisco: Harper & Row, 1979), 77.

backward and forward. It is to enter into the Scriptures through the door of the one who said, "I am the way and the truth and the life" (John 14:6). To do so is to bask in the glow and glory of the one who is "for us" and not "against us" (Rom. 8:31); a God who is "the LORD, the LORD, the compassionate and gracious God, slow to anger, abounding in love and faithfulness, maintaining love to thousands, and forgiving wickedness, rebellion and sin" (Ex. 34:6–7); a God who has predestined us "to be conformed to the likeness of his Son" (Rom. 8:29); a God who is ontologically, essentially, and fundamentally *agapē* ("love"; see 1 John 4:8, 16).

There is a scarlet threat that runs through the Old and New Testaments, that ties together the beginning and the end, and that discloses God's fundamental character. It is not *ḥerem* but the cross. Its dominant apocalyptic symbol is not that of a lion or a wolf or a viper, but rather "the Lamb that was slain from the creation of the world" (Rev. 13:8). With John we testify: "We have seen his glory, the glory of the One and Only, who came from the Father, full of grace and truth" (John 1:14).

A RESPONSE TO
TREMPER LONGMAN III

Eugene H. Merrill

Let me begin by commending Professor Longman for the lucid, engaging, and compelling case he makes for his understanding of the issue that this volume addresses, a case with which I am in substantial agreement. I am particularly appreciative of his sensitivity to the unity of the biblical revelation, which, among other things, demands that the God of the Old Testament be the God of the New Testament, the historical uniqueness of Old Testament holy war notwithstanding. The following response, then, deals mainly with differences in detail and not with major paradigmatic conceptions.

Sacred space and holy war. Longman begins by drawing attention to two ways in which biblical ideology is analogous to that of the extremist Islamic ideology of Osama bin Laden, namely, sacred space and *herem* warfare. By sacred space, he means the areas around Mecca and Medina that have been expanded to include all of Saudi Arabia. Thus, part of bin Laden's agenda is the expulsion of all Westerners from that country because of their contamination of that holy region. This, Longman suggests, is akin to the notion that the tabernacle and temple of ancient Israel were also surrounded by sacred space, violation of which could and did incur the wrath of a holy God.

The emphasis on the concept of sacred space is much appreciated since it is, for the most part, sadly lacking in nonliturgical evangelical settings. The idea that God is in his holy temple and that all the earth should be silent before him is one that needs to be revived. However, the analogy between bin Laden's insistence that Saudi Arabia and other areas must be freed from infidel pollution on the one hand, and the application of Canaanite genocide by Israel on the other, seems a little far-fetched, since Canaan is never explicitly described as sacred space. The stated reason for the prosecution of holy war in Canaan was the removal of the Canaanite nations in order to free up space for Israel's occupation, and the destruction of pagan religious paraphernalia and practices was to eliminate their being inducements to Israelite idolatry (Deut. 7:1–5).

Furthermore, bin Laden's *jihad* is focused on America, the "great Satan," and has little or no territorial concerns. It is blind rage against a perceived cultural imperialism, a terrorist crusade that responsible Muslim spokespersons repudiate precisely because (they say) it violates central tenets of their faith.

The definition of holy war. As Longman points out, the term *ḥerem* is "notoriously hard to translate," and, it might be added, the related term *holy war* is notoriously difficult to define. In its broadest sense, all war is holy war (or, more properly, Yahweh war), for God as sovereign of history concerns himself with all that transpires. More narrowly, holy war is any kind of conflict in which Yahweh is explicitly identified as a protagonist for or against his people Israel. But in line with the theme of this book—namely, the implementation of a policy of genocide conceived and carried out by Yahweh and one that incorporated *ḥerem* as a sine qua non—Professor Longman's examples appear to be much too broad. That is, he makes use of the term *holy war* to describe a course of action in which *ḥerem* never occurs even by implication.

It is not possible to comment on all such examples, but the following are illustrative. In 1 Samuel 23:1–6, David achieves great victory over the Philistines at Keilah, and though some of the features commonly associated with holy war occur in the narrative (e.g., inquiring of Yahweh and the promise of his help), the battle does not result in *ḥerem*. The same is true of the Gibeonite fiasco (Josh. 9), where the only hint of holy war is Israel's carelessness in not inquiring of the Lord (9:14). Second Samuel 11 fares no better as an example. There are, to be sure, holy-war elements (the presence of the ark and the need for ritual purity), but these without *herem* are insufficient to qualify the Ammonite campaign as genocide.

What is particularly puzzling is Professor Longman's consistent application of the term *herem* warfare even to battle narratives where *herem* per se is not mentioned. Justification for this is his admission that "we have been using *herem* as a term to describe the waging of war in Israel, in essence as a synonym for holy war or Yahweh war." But he then goes on to make the very distinction that we feel needs to be made, namely, that "in actuality, *herem* refers to the climactic aspect of divine warfare: the offering of the conquered people and their possessions to the Lord." It is precisely that "climactic aspect" that is lacking in most of Longman's examples.

The New Testament examples fare little better. It seems somewhat of a stretch to regard Jesus' exorcisms, for instance, as *herem* war or even as holy war. The same is true of Paul's assessment of our Lord's victorious engagement with the forces of evil on the cross (Col. 2:13–15). Likewise, one is hard pressed to see *herem* in the triumphant ascension of Christ as described by Paul in his allusion to Psalm 68 in Ephesians 4:8.

When he turns to the New Testament apocalyptic texts, however, Longman makes an overwhelmingly convincing case of *herem* war at the end of the age. He cites especially Revelation 19:11–21, and though he describes the scene there as "a highly symbolic description of the final judgment," he leaves no doubt as to its historical factuality. He correctly connects the coming of Jesus as divine warrior with holy-war passages from the Old Testament and with his violent opposition to and conquest of the "unholy warrior known as the beast in Revelation 13:1–10." In this manner, the New Testament gives evidence of a holy-war continuity with the Old.

Conclusion. On the whole, Professor Longman has moved the discussion of Old Testament holy war forward in a most persuasive and helpful manner. The response offered here has more to do with fine points of definition than with his overall argument for spiritual continuity of the theme of holy war from the Old Testament to the New. I find myself in substantial agreement with those parts of his presentation that address the core issues.

Two points that he stresses seem worthy to be repeated here: the insistence that the God of the Old Testament is the God of the New, even in his role as divine warrior; and the linkage between the application of *ḥerem* to the historical Canaanites and to the eschatological nations who have proven to be irremediably unrepentant and therefore rightfully condemned to everlasting destruction. Citing Meredith Kline's concept of "intrusion ethics,"[1] Longman observes that "we should not be amazed that God ordered the death of the Canaanites, but rather we should stand in amazement *that he lets anyone live.* The Conquest [of Canaan] involves the intrusion of the ethics of the end times, the consummation, into the period of common grace. In a sense, the destruction of the Canaanites is a preview of the final judgment" (emphasis his). With this hermeneutic of holy war we find ourselves in hearty agreement.

---

[1]Meredith G. Kline, *The Structure of Biblical Authority* (Grand Rapids: Eerdmans, 1972).

A RESPONSE TO TREMPER LONGMAN III

Daniel L. Gard

Tremper Longman's analysis of the topic is perhaps the closest to my own. Although his understanding of the mode of continuity has, in this book, been labeled as "spiritual," its most stunning manifestation is "eschatological." My own reading of Longman's contribution is thus largely one of agreement. However, there are a few somewhat minor points I would raise as needing further reflection and thought among the Christian communities.

(1) I wonder if contemporary terrorists such as bin Laden have in fact extended Old Testament (or even Qurʾanic) concepts of sacred space to the peninsula of Saudi Arabia. Surely Islam holds that Mecca and Medina are holy places and, at the same time, holds the Old Testament to be a kind of Scripture. But there is no evidence in bin Laden's actions or words that Old Testament warfare and his own *jihad* have direct links. Religion has become the self-justification for bin Laden and other terrorists, but at heart their motives are more political than religious.

This is significant largely for our theological understanding of the acts of bin Laden and other modern executioners of genocide. I would argue that bin Laden's brand of Islam, like some branches of Christianity, misidentifies the relationship between the kingdom of God and earthly principalities. Those who would kill human beings in the name of God have taken upon themselves and their political constituency a role reserved in the New Testament for the state, not the people of God. I have argued in my own article that ancient Israel was uniquely church and state, a status that can be claimed by *no other political entity*. This is not an unusual misidentification, as Christian history itself gives evidence (the Crusades or the Inquisition, to name but two).

I raise this issue not to criticize Longman's fine contribution but rather to supplement his analysis by suggesting that the relationship between church and state is radically different for ancient Israel than for any other nation. What is said of bin Laden's Islam is just as validly said of "Christianity's lunatic fringe," which, of course, Longman precisely does.

(2) Tremper Longman raises a salient point regarding what is often a difficult reality for Christian readers of the Old Testament. He states, regarding Jericho and Ai:

> In conclusion, we must point out that the Bible does not understand the destruction of the men, women, and children of these cities as a slaughter of innocents. Not even the children are considered innocent. They are all part of an inherently wicked culture that, if allowed to live, would morally and theologically pollute the people of Israel.

This theological observation is precisely that classic Christian anthropology expressed in the doctrine of original sin. The amazing thing is not that Jericho and Ai were destroyed. The amazing thing is that all humanity, including ancient Israel and every other child of Adam, has not been destroyed. For those who hold that baptism is the sacrament of regeneration, the inclusion of even children in the necessity for baptism is apparent. In the end, all those who are outside of Christ will meet the same fate as the adults and infants of Jericho and Ai. Only God's monergistic covenant can alter that fate. Whether Canaanite, Israelite, or Gentile Christian, all are sinners and stand under a sentence of death.

(3) Of course, Longman himself emphatically states the idea that it is by grace that anyone lives. Working with the "intrusion ethics" of Meredith Kline, he begins the process of understanding the discussion of Canaanite genocide from the perspective

of grace. With the restrictions of space, it is understandable that Longman cannot fully deal with the issue he raises about "how a loving God can exercise any kind of penalty toward the wicked."

Perhaps a starting point for further discussion and reflection has to do with the nature of God himself. Among his attributes is that he is both loving and just. Typically, popular theological thought tends to make the two mutually exclusive. If God is love, how can he exercise justice, especially if that decree of justice seems to contradict what we perceive as "love"? Here I would suggest that the apparent conflict has more to do with our limitations as humans than with any real conflict. Both his love and his justice are real and pure.

Thus, Kline's "intrusion ethics" and its understanding of the Old Testament destruction of the Canaanites as the final judgment foreshadowed is extraordinarily helpful in coming to grips with what is for many an ethical quandary. God's justice will be manifested before the universe on the Last Day, just as it was against the Canaanites. But those with whom God has established his covenant of grace will live. Is God unjust in preserving the Israelites and destroying the Canaanites, especially since all have sinned and equally deserve condemnation? If it appears so, the issue is not one of God's justice but of human fallibility and inability fully to comprehend the ways of God.

To express the ethical dilemma another way, I would borrow a question from historic Lutheran theology (whether other theological systems struggle with this, I am not sure). That question is: Why is one person saved and another not? Is it because there exists in God himself a love of one person but a hatred of another, and therefore he saves the one he loves and destroys the one he hates? Such a position contradicts the clear biblical position that God desires for all people to be saved. Or is it because there is a distinction between the two persons? One perhaps seeks God, and the other does not. Here, too, is a conflict with the teaching of the Bible. After all, does not Scripture teach that all have sinned? Are there any who do righteously?

The question as to why one person is saved and another not is simply unanswerable, and for that reason it has been called the "cross of the theologian." Longman wisely avoids answering the question in its permutation arising from the disturbing question, "Why the Canaanites? . . . Here, like Job, we are left unanswered as to why suffering comes to one and not another." This is a paradox of biblical theology, especially acute when Scripture itself does not provide an answer to the question. In my opinion, the Christian thinker must simply be silent, as God is silent. In so doing, we can maintain that his righteous justice and his compassionate love are both true.

(4) I especially appreciate Longman's simple and clear dealing with the relevant Old Testament texts. There are a few points, however, that merit further discussion. For example, was Uriah's refusal to sleep with his wife really grounded in Israelite Scripture (Lev. 15:11–18) and not in what Longman refers to as "typical warrior's bravado"? Uriah's stated reason for his refusal is not the cultic code but rather the comparative living conditions of his comrades as well as the ark itself being in a tent (2 Sam. 11:11). Much of the ancient Near East held similar warfare codes, and Uriah's Hittite background could well have been motivation enough for his refusal. If so, the contrast between the Hittite Uriah and the Israelite King David is even more pronounced. Uriah operated from a higher ethic than David despite the fact that David had Yahweh's own revealed Word.

Longman's article tends to emphasize the cooperative nature of Israel's warfare rather than those incidents in which Yahweh fights without human cooperation. The majority of texts, in fact, do speak of these wars as synergistic, that is, as a cooperative effort on the part of the Lord and Israel. Still, there are significant texts that attribute warfare victory to the Lord alone (see especially Ex. 15:1–21; 2 Chron. 20; 32); that is, they are monergistic (the Lord fighting alone without human cooperation). In still other cases, Yahweh fights alongside his angels, a scenario taken up by apocalyptic literature and found in New Testament descriptions of the final eschatological victory.

(5) One final point might be made. In Longman's discussion of "Phase 5: The Final Battle," he states that "when Jesus returns again, he will complete the victory assured by his death on the cross." Here, I would suggest that we think not of Jesus' return as the completion of his victory won at Calvary; rather, Easter is the completion of that victory. It is at Easter that sin and death and hell were defeated. In other words, the victory is already won. The Last Day and its judgment on the living and

the dead and the final imposition of *ḥerem* is the manifestation of the victory won at Calvary and sealed on Easter.

My reactions to Tremper Longman's article are overwhelmingly positive. There are points in which I find disagreement, although they are more points of emphasis rather than direction. I thank him for his insightful work.

SCRIPTURE INDEX

SUBJECT INDEX

Are Miraculous Gifts for Today?

Four Views

Wayne A. Grudem, General Editor

Do you fully understand your own position and the positions of others on whether the gifts of tongues, prophecy, and healing are for today? Cessationists say *no*. Pentecostal, Charismatic, and Third Wave Christians say *yes*. Open-But-Cautious evangelicals say *maybe*.

In this book, general editor Wayne A. Grudem moderates a spirited conversation, providing an impartial forum for comparing the four main lines of thinking: Cessationist, represented by Richard B. Gaffin Jr.; Open But Cautious (Robert L. Saucy); Third Wave (C. Samuel Storms); and Pentecostal/Charismatic (Douglas A. Oss).

ISBN 978-0-310-20155-7

Also Available in the Counterpoints Series:

Four Views on the Book of Revelation

Is the book of Revelation a prophecy fulfilled when the temple fell in a.d. 70, a metaphor for the battle between good and evil raging until Christ's return, a chronological record of events between Christ's ascension and the new heaven and new earth, or an already/not yet prophetic dichotomy of fulfillment and waiting?

Four Views on the Book of Revelation will expand your understanding of the Bible's most mystifying book, and it may even change your mind.

Moody Bible Institute professor C. Marvin Pate mediates the lively dialogue and adds his own view to those of Kenneth L. Gentry Jr., Sam Hamstra Jr., and Robert L. Thomas.

ISBN 978-0-310-21080-1

Three Views on the Millennium and Beyond

Sort through the three major perspectives to draw your own conclusion about the Millennium and its relationship with other eschatological events.

Premillennialism says it's a literal, one-thousand-year earthly reign of Christ, which occurs sometime after the Rapture but before Christ's final return.

Postmillennialism says it's a one-thousand-year period before Christ comes back when the majority of people on earth acknowledge his reign over all things.

Amillennialism contends that it's a metaphor for the time between Christ's ascension and his final return to usher in the kingdom of God.

Craig A. Blaising, Kenneth L. Gentry Jr., and Robert B. Strimple defend their positions and respond to the others. General editor Darrel L. Bock summarizes the main issues of difference among them.

ISBN 978-0-310-20143-4

Four Views on Salvation in a Pluralistic World

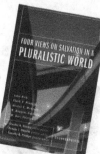

If you've ever asked:

- What is the eternal fate of indigenous people Christian missionaries have not reached with the gospel?
- How could believing in Christ not be essential for salvation when Jesus said, "No one can come to the Father except through me"?

then you need to read this Counterpoints volume.

John Hick, Clark Pinnock, Alister E. McGrath, R. Douglas Geivett, and W. Gary Phillips defend their positions on the most challenged belief in western Christianity. Dennis L. Okholm and Timothy R. Phillips are the general editors.

ISBN 978-0-310-21276-8

Three Views on Creation and Evolution

Separate the hard evidence from emotional rhetoric in the debate over origins. Noted evangelical Christian authorities John Mark Reynolds and Paul Nelson (Young Earth Creationism), Robert C. Newman (Progressive [Old Earth] Creationism), and Howard J. Van Till (Fully Gifted Creation [Theistic Evolution]) represent their positions and discuss the underlying philosophical and theological questions that make this such a critical issue.

Adding to the participant dialogue, representative scholars from theology, biblical studies, philosophy, and science analyze each essay with insight from their respective disciplines. Well-known author Phillip E. Johnson and Stanford scientist Richard H. Bube summarize the discussion into its key points, providing a starting point for further research. J. P. Moreland and John Mark Reynolds are the general editors.

ISBN 978-0-310-22017-6

Five Views on Sanctification

Five Views on Sanctification will deepen your understanding of the moral perfection of Christ as it presents differing ideas about how that perfection affects the Christian life.

Can we live up to the Wesleyan ideal of "entire sanctification" held by Melvin E. Dieter, or are Reformed scholars like Anthony J. Hoekema correct that complete holiness in this life is impossible? What roles do the transforming gifts of the Holy Spirit play, according to Pentecostals like Stanley M. Horton? What is the Keswick tradition of J. Robertson McQuilkin, and what wisdom on this issue has John F. Walvoord found in the writings of St. Augustine?

ISBN 978-0-310-21269-0

Three Views on the Rapture

Eschatology doesn't end when you decide how to approach the book of Revelation. If you believe in a premillennial rapture, you want to know whether it happens before, during, or after the Great Tribulation.

Richard R. Reiter introduces *Three Views on the Rapture* (formerly titled *The Rapture*) with an essay tracing the history of this debate in American evangelicalism. Gleason L. Archer Jr., Paul D. Feinberg, and Douglas J. Moo each represent and defend one of the views.

ISBN 978-0-310-21298-0

Five Views on Law and Gospel

Examine the relevance of the Old Testament law to Christian living with five scholars represent- ing the most common evangelical Christian views.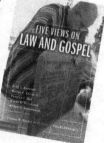

Douglas J. Moo presents a modified Lutheran answer; Wayne G. Strickland de- fends the Dispensational view; while Walter C. Kaiser Jr. argues that the "weightier issues" of the Mosaic Law still apply to Christians. Willem A. VanGemeren and Greg L. Bahnsen present Theonomic and Non-theonomic Reformed points of view.

ISBN 978-0-310-21271-3

Four Views on Hell

Learn why not everyone agrees that a hell of fire and sulfur exists or that the unsaved will suffer there forever. Leading scholars discuss whether hell is a literal fire, a metaphor for separation from God, a purgatorial place of purification, or a place of temporary pun- ishment for those who have not accepted Christ.

Contributors include John F. Walvoord, William V. Crockett, Zachary J. Hayes, and Clark H. Pinnock. William Crockett serves as the general editor.

ISBN 978-0-310-21268-3